e t

ERS

Swindon
BOROUGH COUNCIL

The
History
Press

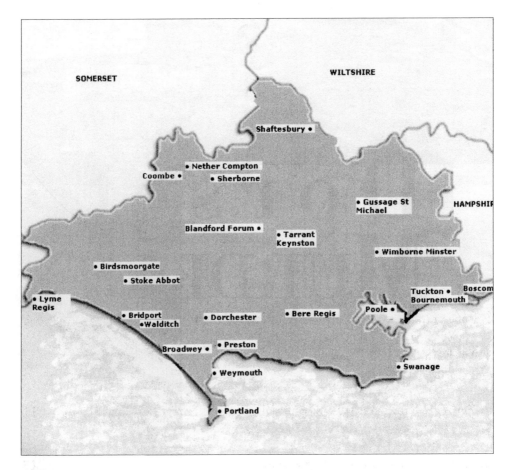

Map of Dorset.

First published 2008

The History Press Ltd
The Mill, Brimscombe Port
Stroud, Gloucestershire, GL5 2QG
www.thehistorypress.co.uk

© Nicola Sly, 2008

The right of Nicola Sly to be identified as the Author
of this work has been asserted in accordance with the
Copyrights, Designs and Patents Act 1988.

British Library Cataloguing in Publication Data.
A catalogue record for this book is available from the British Library.

ISBN 978 0 7509 5107 4

Typesetting and origination by The History Press Ltd.
Printed in Great Britain

CONTENTS

AUTHOR'S NOTE & ACKNOWLEDGEMENTS

When I was asked to compile a collection of Dorset murders, I was instantly faced with a dilemma – what to do about Bournemouth? Prior to boundary changes in 1974, Bournemouth was located in Hampshire and, since all the murders in this selection occurred before this date, five of those included in this book were technically committed in Hampshire rather than in Dorset. In the end it was the cases themselves which swayed my decision to write about the county of Dorset as it is today. Four of the cases were nationally notorious and the fifth – the story of the Wright family – was one of the most tragic I have ever come across in an almost thirty-year-long study of murder.

Thus the murders of Emma Sherriff in 1908, Irene Wilkins in 1921 and Francis Rattenbury in 1935 are included, as are the infamous crimes of Neville Heath, which took place in both London and Bournemouth. They join a diverse collection of murders committed for financial gain, for revenge, or for ridding the killer of a partner who, for one reason or another, had simply become a nuisance. Some of the murders can be attributed to the insanity of the killer, while others, such as the mysterious murder at the Coverdale Kennels, remain unsolved to this day.

There are numerous people who must be acknowledged and thanked for their assistance in compiling this collection. John J. Eddleston, Roger Guttridge and Theresa Murphy have all previously published books either on murder in Dorset or more general reference works on British murders and executions. The memoirs of J.D. Casswell QC, who defended or prosecuted some of the accused, provided a fascinating behind-the-scenes insight into their cases, while Douglas Browne and E.V. Tullett's book on the life and cases of Sir Bernard Spilsbury gave a new depth to the meticulous work of the celebrated pathologist. These books are recorded in more detail in the bibliography, as are the local and national newspapers, which proved an invaluable source of material. My thanks must also go to the staff of the Dorset History Centre for their help in my research and to the *Daily Echo*, Bournemouth, for permission to use photographs from their archives.

I must also thank John Van der Kiste and, of course, my husband, Richard, without whom this book could not have been written. His suggestions for improving each chapter were invaluable, as was his help with the photography. Both he and my father, John Higginson, have supported me from the first word of this book to the last.

Finally, my thanks must go to my editor at The History Press, Matilda Richards, for her continued help and encouragement.

1

'I WILL BE DAMNED IF I KNOW HER A MAN FROM A WOMAN'

Bere Regis, 1818

At about 10 p.m. on 14 May 1818, Ann Loveridge was standing on her front doorstep taking a breath of fresh air when she suddenly heard a woman's voice cry out, 'Oh! The Lord have mercy on me!' A low groan followed, then silence. Ann called out to her next-door neighbour, Elizabeth Rose, to ask if she had heard anything, but she hadn't.

The noises had seemed to come from the direction of the home of another neighbour, Priscilla Brown, who lived with her eight-year-old son Charles in a cottage some twenty yards away. Ann Loveidge had a quick look around the area but saw nothing out of the ordinary.

An hour later, labourer Robert Lane was walking down Back Lane, the small road that ran behind Priscilla Brown's cottage, when he spotted a woman he recognised as Priscilla lying on her back on a dung heap. Thinking that she may have had a seizure, he spoke to her three times. Having received no response, he placed his hand on her breast to see if he could detect a heartbeat and, when he could find none, he ran to get help.

The first people to arrive on the scene were Priscilla's brother and a neighbour, Henry Philips. Between them, the men carried Priscilla back to her house, still unsure of whether she was dead or just unconscious. A doctor was summoned, but by the time Dr Thomas Nott arrived at 1 a.m. on the morning of 15 May, they had all realised that it was the former.

West Street, Bere Regis, 1920s.

There were a number of people milling about Priscilla's small cottage by then and the doctor was only able to give the body a cursory examination, at which he noted that the woman's throat was blackened and that she had marks around her mouth and nose. Dr Nott came to the conclusion that the woman had been strangled, but when he was able to conduct a more detailed post-mortem examination later that morning, during which he opened the body and head of the victim, he realised that the cause of death had been suffocation rather than strangulation. It seemed as though someone had obstructed Priscilla Brown's nose and mouth, probably with a hand, and prevented her from breathing. Dr Nott also confirmed that Brown was between six and seven months pregnant.

The police began investigations into the murder and soon had a prime suspect. Everyone in the village knew that Priscilla Brown was pregnant and the father of her unborn child was rumoured to be John Gallop, a twenty-nine-year-old labourer who had recently married and now lived in lodgings just outside the village with his new wife.

In the course of their enquiries, police found a lot of villagers who had something to tell them about Gallop. Farmer Thomas Homer had seen John Gallop walk past his house at between 9 p.m. and 10 p.m. on the night of 14 May, heading in the direction of Priscilla's house, which was about 100 yards away. Gallop had been walking at a steady pace, swinging a walking stick and wearing a rough, long brown greatcoat. Homer had seen Gallop pass by again on his return journey some fifteen minutes later, again walking at the same unhurried pace. Another witness, John Sexey, who lived nearby had also seen Gallop going towards, and then later away from Priscilla Brown's cottage on the night of the murder.

Gallop's landlord, Benjamin Romain, told police that Gallop had left his house at about 8 p.m. on the night of 14 May and walked off in the direction of Bere Regis village. Romain went to bed at about 10.30 p.m. but did not fall asleep immediately. He had not heard Gallop returning.

As the prime suspect – and in fact the only suspect – police wasted no time in arresting John Gallop and charging him with the wilful murder of Priscilla Brown. As he was taken away, Romain later testified in court that Gallop had whispered to him, 'Say I was in bed for ten o'clock'.

Tried for the murder at the Dorset Assizes, before Mr Justice Burrough, John Gallop pleaded 'Not Guilty', denying all knowledge of the murder and also denying being the father of Priscilla Brown's unborn child.

The first witness to be called was eight-year-old Charles Brown who, after being tested on his ability to differentiate between the truth and lies, identified John Gallop by pointing to him in the courtroom. He testified that he knew the accused because he had often visited his mother's house. On the night of the murder, he told the court that stones had been thrown against the cottage doors three times. His mother had gone first to the front door, then to the back, to try and establish where the noise was coming from. At the back door she spoke to Gallop, then, without pausing to put on her bonnet, she went out into the back garden and walked towards Back Lane. She hadn't come back until she was brought back dead. Charles talked of hearing Gallop's voice calling him out into the garden, but said that he hadn't gone because he couldn't tell what Gallop had said.

At this, Gallop interjected, saying that the boy had said before that he had never heard any voice, and that Thomas Clinch had heard him say this. Mr Justice Burrough asked Charles about what he had heard several times, but he continued to insist that he had recognised Gallop's voice calling him. Eventually the judge decided to ask Thomas Clinch for his version of events.

However, the decision to name Clinch as a witness backfired for John Gallop, since Clinch promptly testified that he had indeed heard young Charles say that someone had flung stones at the door and that he had later heard Gallop's voice. Far from contradicting Charles Brown's testimony, Clinch's evidence actually corroborated it.

The arguments by Gallop against Charles Brown's testimony set a pattern that was to be repeated again and again as different witnesses gave evidence.

Gallop disputed the testimony of Romain, his landlord, saying that Romain had spoken false of him and that he had never asked him to say that he was in bed by ten o'clock.

Several people came forward to say that Gallop had spoken about murdering Priscilla Brown before the event. Page Ross, a servant, spoke of meeting Gallop in Homer's barn on 1 May and of Gallop asking him if he had heard any rumours. When Ross said he hadn't, Gallop told him, 'They have got it about town that Cil Brown is with child by me, but I will be damned if I know her a man from a woman. And if she swears it to me, damn my eyes if I will not murder her the next minute.'

Predictably, Gallop immediately protested. 'He has sworn false against me. I never said I would murder her and you may depend on it, my Lord'. Yet if Ross had lied, so too did

Thomas Strickland, for he had also heard Gallop's threats and his statement matched Ross's word for word.

Elizabeth Harris was another witness who, according to Gallop, 'swore false'. She had been working in the fields with Gallop during the previous year when Gallop had bragged before her and several other witnesses that he could kill a person in five minutes without being discovered. Harris asked him how he would do that and Gallop responded by placing one hand around her throat and the other across her nose and mouth, pinching her nostrils closed.

'Did he hurt you materially?' asked the judge.

'Oh yes, my Lord', replied Harris, adding somewhat unnecessarily, 'But he didn't kill me.'

Gallop protested once more. 'She has a spite against me, and every word she has spoken is false.'

The court heard from Thomas Homer, John Sexey and another witness, Sarah Welch, who had all seen John Gallop walking either towards or away from Priscilla Brown's home on the night of 14 May. Perhaps not surprisingly, according to Gallop all were lying.

Finally, Gallop himself took the witness stand. He made a great show of dismissing almost every word of evidence given in court so far as lies and gave a detailed account of his movements on the night of 14 May, which, of course, did not include being anywhere near the home of Priscilla Brown. Yet although he insisted that he had an alibi for the entire evening, Gallop was unable to name any person who might have corroborated his story.

It was left to his defence counsel to try and repair some of the damage caused by Gallop's testimony, which he attempted to do by calling two or three character witnesses for his client. In hindsight, this was perhaps not such a good idea, since none of the witnesses seemed to know Gallop too well and had very little good to say about him.

The jury retired for only a few minutes before returning with a verdict of 'Guilty', leaving the judge to pronounce the prescribed sentence of death. Calling the murder one of the foulest crimes he had heard, he urged John Gallop to fall to his knees after leaving court and endeavour by prayer and supplication to obtain forgiveness from a merciful God.

Gallop accepted the sentence with apparent indifference and, after leaving the dock, continued to protest that he was as innocent of the murder as a newborn baby. It is not known whether or not he heeded the judge's advice to pray for forgiveness, but regardless, he did not have long to wait before meeting his maker. He was hanged at Dorchester on 27 July 1818 and his body was then anatomised.

2

'THE HORSE HAVE KICKED POOR JOHN AND KILLED 'EE'

Birdsmoorgate, 1856

Nearing her fortieth birthday, Elizabeth Martha Brown was, by nineteenth-century standards, well past her prime. Yet she was still an attractive looking woman, with a head of beautiful curly hair, sufficiently so to attract the attentions of a much younger man. The fact that she had also managed to save almost £50 – the equivalent of more than £3,000 today – could, of course, have added to her appeal.

Martha, as she was usually known, met nineteen-year-old John Anthony Brown when he came to work on the farm where she was employed as a servant. The couple soon became lovers and eventually married, leaving their employ to live in a small cottage in Birdsmoorgate near Beaminster. John set himself up as a carrier while Martha ran a small grocery shop from her home and looked after their one child. However, the marriage was not a happy one. John spent long hours away on business, frequently arriving home drunk very late at night. In addition, Martha was suspicious that his relationship with Mary Davies, the wife of the village butcher, was an improper one, and, according to some contemporary newspaper reports, she once actually caught the couple in bed together. Whether or not these reports are accurate, Martha was certainly a jealous woman.

On 5 July 1856, George Fooks, a carrier from nearby Blackdown and a long-term acquaintance of John's, joined him at home for breakfast. Having eaten, the two men loaded their horse-drawn wagons and, at nine o'clock, set off to deliver their loads to Beaminster. Within half a mile, Mary Davies joined them and walked alongside the carts for a short while before leaving to go to her job as a washerwoman.

View of Beaminster village, 1920s.

The two carriers arrived at Beaminster, unloaded their carts and began the return journey. When they reached Broadwindsor, they stopped for refreshments at an inn. While there, they divided some money they had earned together, then went into the skittle alley, where they stayed drinking beer and playing skittles until half-past eleven at night.

They resumed their journey, with Brown calling at a saddler's in Broadwindsor to collect a mill belt, which he placed on his wagon. The two men came to Mount Corner, where their routes home parted, shortly before midnight. According to Fooks, Brown was 'a little in liquor', but not obviously drunk and certainly capable of taking care of himself.

What happened next is uncertain, since the only account of the following few hours is that given by Martha Brown. She claimed that she found her husband lying unconscious on the doorstep at two o'clock the following morning and had, with difficulty, dragged him into the cottage, where he had clutched tightly at her skirts for several hours and refused to let her go to summon a doctor.

She finally managed to escape her husband's grasp at five o'clock in the morning and ran to the home of John's cousin, Richard Damon, who lived nearby. Banging on Damon's door, she had begged him to come to her house as the horse had kicked John and injured him.

Damon found Brown lying on the floor of his cottage, a handkerchief bound round his head. There was a pool of blood on the floor behind him and his hair was matted with blood and brain tissue. Damon picked up his cousin's limp hand and found it cold – John Brown was dead. When he broke this news to Martha, her only response was to ask, 'Is he?' Moments later she asked Damon to go and call Harriet Knight.

Damon did as she asked, then went straight to the field where he knew that Brown normally kept his horse. There he found the horse safely locked in its stable. His cousin's hat was standing against the gatepost on its crown. There was a little vomit on the ground near to where the hat was found and marks in the roadside dust, which seemed to indicate that a man had fallen to his knees there. The gate was closed and latched and the horse's halter lay just inside it, beneath the rail of a hayrick.

Having picked up the hat and noticed that it was undamaged and unmarked by blood, Damon returned to his cousin's home, stopping on the way to summon help from numerous villagers. He arrived back in the company of the village publican, Mr Stanton, Joseph Davies (husband of Mary) and Francis Turner, Brown's next-door neighbour. They were greeted by Martha, who told them, 'The horse have kicked poor John and killed 'ee' [*sic*].

The men examined the dead body and noted the presence of a great many wounds on John Brown's head. One of his boots was unlaced and one hand was bent at a strange angle. They looked for evidence of blood in the passageway, along which Martha would have helped her husband, and also in the road outside the cottage, but found none.

Martha continued to repeat her account of her husband being kicked by his horse. George Fooks, who arrived later that morning, asked if Brown had managed to say anything before he died. According to Martha, he had pointed to his head and said simply, 'the horse'. She told Fooks that she had sat on the floor cradling her husband's head from two o'clock onwards, while he clung to her waist. She had only managed to escape to summon help when he grew weak and fainted.

Initially, Martha's account of events was believed. The horse was known to be a particularly vicious animal and Brown's frequent drunkenness was also legendary in the area. However, Brown had several wounds to his head which had completely smashed his skull like an eggshell. In addition, the horse had been locked in its stable and, in spite of the fact that Brown had lost a great deal of blood, no traces whatsoever had been found outside the house. At the inquest, held at the Rose and Crown public house in Birdsmoorgate, it was pointed out that blood and brain matter were found adhering to the walls of the room in the cottage in which the body lay.

Richard Broster and Joachim Gilbert, the two surgeons from Beaminster who had carried out the post-mortem examination, testified to the extent of Brown's wounds. He had a broken nose and a triangular wound above his left eyebrow, through which the bone of his skull protruded. A further cut adjacent to his left eye ran vertically down his face and there were numerous separate injuries to the top and back of his head, as well as a fracture to the front of the skull. In total, seven pieces of bone, from half an inch to three inches long had been driven into his brain, which had bled extensively. At least three of the blows to Brown's head were judged sufficiently severe to cause his death and, in the opinion of the surgeons, the damage to his brain was so great that, after the first blow, he would have been instantly paralysed. There was absolutely no possibility that he could have crawled, or even spoken, after being hit. In addition, both of the medical witnesses felt that the injuries – particularly the broken nose – would have bled profusely and there would certainly have been copious quantities of blood on the road and on Brown's doorstep had his death occurred in the manner related by Martha.

They also believed that Brown would have been unable to grip his wife and thus could not have prevented her from going for help.

The jury at the inquest recorded a verdict of wilful murder by person or persons unknown and, given the rumoured unhappy state of the Brown's marriage, Martha was the most obvious suspect. In due course she was arrested for the murder of her husband and committed by local magistrates to Dorchester Gaol to await her trial at the next Assizes.

Her trial opened at Dorchester on 21 July 1856 and Martha showed no emotion as she pleaded 'Not Guilty'.

Counsel for the prosecution, Mr Stock, acknowledged that the evidence against her was entirely circumstantial. He instructed the jury to weigh up these circumstances carefully before arriving at their verdict.

Harriet Knight, the woman Martha had wanted Damon to fetch, lived near to the gate of the field where John Brown kept his horse. She told the court that she had heard the field gate slam closed at about 2 a.m. on the morning of Brown's death, followed by the sound of a horse grazing and footsteps leading towards the Brown's cottage. Although she had not checked, she believed those footsteps to have been John Brown's. Another villager, Mrs Frampton, told of hearing a frightful scream coming from the direction of the Brown's home at around 2 a.m.

The court heard evidence from Richard Damon, George Fooks and Francis Turner, who all described what they had found when they went to Brown's house on the morning of his death. The curate of Broadwindsor, the Revd Augustus Newland de la Foss, also addressed the court. He spoke of accompanying Brown's mother to the house two days after the death of her son, describing how she fainted into his arms when she went into the room where his body lay in its coffin. Everyone who had been in the room at the time had been grief-stricken and emotional, with the sole exception of Martha Brown.

According to Revd de la Foss, Martha had told him that she was accused of murdering her husband but was as innocent as the angels in heaven. When de la Foss remarked that all the evidence pointed to Brown having met his death in that very room, Martha assured him that blood would be found outside and also 'the thing it was done with'. She then asked him, 'What should make I kill him to lose my home and have to lie under the hedge?' [sic].

The surgeons then repeated the evidence they had given at the inquest, adding that they were of the opinion that the wounds to Brown's head had been caused by blows from a blunt instrument, such as a hatchet, rather than resulting from a kick or kicks by a horse. Mr Broster told the court that he had examined the horse's shoes and, although he found one shoe to be in two pieces, he still didn't believe that the horse had kicked Brown. Questions were asked in court about a hatchet that John Brown was known to have owned, which had disappeared since the murder. Both Richard Damon and the local police had searched high and low for it, but it could not be found.

Damon's wife provided the court with a motive for the murder, describing Martha's intense jealousy of Mary Davies, a woman Martha consistently referred to as 'an old bitch'.

Martha Brown did not enter the witness box since her defence counsel, Mr Edwards, was undoubtedly wary about what might be revealed under cross-examination by the prosecution. In fact, Edwards called just one witness, Martha's previous employer, Mr Symes, who supplied a character witness for her, describing her as 'as kind and inoffensive a woman as ever lived'.

Edwards concentrated his defence on showing that the evidence against his client was purely circumstantial. He complained that nothing had been said about a hatchet until that day – if it had been mentioned before, then Martha might have been able to produce it.

He dismissed the evidence suggesting that Martha and John had not lived together in harmony and pooh-poohed the notion that Martha was jealous of Mary Davies. He pointed out that, far from thinking of murdering her husband, on the night of his death she had been concerned only with his comfort.

Addressing the question of the lack of blood, Edwards pointed out that Martha had already told police that her husband had bled copiously onto her apron. He could find nothing to suggest that a search for the apron in question had ever been conducted.

Edwards also suggested to the court that it was not Martha who was responsible for the theory that the horse had killed her husband, but visitors to the house after his death. He also maintained that a person would need great strength to inflict such serious wounds and that Martha would simply not have been strong enough.

Finally, he challenged the medical evidence, stating that the doctors freely admitted that they had seen cases before where a patient had received what should have been a fatal blow on the head, only to live for years afterwards. As one surgeon had put it, 'nature often excited itself in a way that was quite unexpected'. Edwards then put forward the theory that John Brown had been attacked on his doorstep by some other party; someone who knew that he would be carrying money from his day's work.

The jury retired to consider their verdict, returning after almost four hours to enquire whether they might ask some further questions of the medical witnesses. Joachim Gilbert was recalled to the witness box and the jury asked if there would have been any difference to the victim's head wounds had they been examined immediately after the murder, rather than three and a half days later at the post-mortem. Gilbert assured the jury that the time delay had made no difference to the nature of the injuries and also dismissed the idea that the pieces of skull may have been driven into the brain when the body was moved after death. The doctors also refuted the judge's suggestion that Brown's grip on his wife might have been a death grip, saying that, given the extent and seriousness of his wounds, Brown would have been quite incapable of gripping anything or anyone.

It took just a few more minutes of deliberation for the jury to find the accused guilty of the wilful murder of her husband and, with Martha steadfastly protesting her innocence, sentence of death was passed. Before Martha was led from the court to await her execution, Revd de la Foss managed to ask her if the story about the horse was a 'trumped up' one. Martha conceded that it was, but swore that she had never hit her husband. She then stated that he had met his death by falling downstairs.

With the date of her execution set for 9 August 1856, Martha waited until two days before to dictate a statement to the prison governor.

She told of her husband arriving home drunk in the early hours of the morning, his hat missing. When she questioned him as to where he had left it, he responded with a tirade of abuse. He then demanded a drink of cold tea. Martha said she had none, but offered to make him some fresh tea, which prompted a further outburst of shouting and swearing. Martha had then asked him why he was so angry – had he been to see Mary Davies? At this, Brown erupted into violence. He struck her on the side of her head with sufficient force to confuse her, then snatched a horsewhip from the mantelpiece and hit her three times across the shoulders with it. He then said that he hoped he would find her dead in the morning, delivering a final kick to her left side before bending down to unlace his heavy boots.

In a rage at being so abused and beaten, Martha had grabbed John's hatchet and retaliated, striking him several blows on the head. After the first blow, Brown fell to the floor and never moved again. According to Martha, as soon as she had hit him, she would have given the world not to have done it. John had hit her so hard, she said, that she was almost 'out of her senses' and scarcely knew what she was doing.

The then Home Secretary, Sir George Grey, had already received a lengthy petition asking for clemency for Martha Brown but had decided against granting it. In the light of Martha's new statement and the provocation she claimed to have received before killing her husband, the prison chaplain determined to have one last attempt at securing a reprieve.

He hurried to London but was unable to see the Home Secretary in person, Grey being in Ireland at the time. His under-secretary, Mr Waddington, had no means of contacting him and no authority to stay the execution himself. Thus, at 8 a.m. on the morning of 9 August, Martha Brown was escorted to the gallows at Dorchester by two clerics.

Wearing a long black dress, she walked bravely to the gallows and shook hands with the officials. Hangman William Calcraft placed a white hood over her head and strapped her legs together in order to preserve her modesty by preventing her skirt from billowing up as she fell. Her death was not instantaneous and she was seen to struggle briefly before finally dying. After hanging for one hour, the body of Elizabeth Martha Brown was removed from the scaffold and buried within the prison grounds.

A crowd of between 3,000 and 4,000 people watched the execution from a vantage point in North Square. Among the spectators was a youthful Thomas Hardy, on whom the execution had a profound effect. He was still writing about it almost seventy years later and Martha Brown was certainly the inspiration for – if not the subject of – one of his best-known novels, *Tess of the D'Urbervilles*.

[Note: Martha and John's name is sometimes spelled Browne in contemporary accounts of the murder. Likewise, Mary Davies and her husband are sometimes referred to as Davis.]

3

'I FANCIED IT WAS A SORT OF DEATHLY SCREAM'

Stoke Abbott, 1858

This is the account of the murder of Sarah Guppy. Sarah and her mother lodged with a man named James Seal and, by coincidence, the man suspected of murdering her was also called James Seal, although the two men were not related. The accused will be referred to as Jim Seal to differentiate between the two men.

Sarah Ann Guppy lived at Buckshorn House, which was situated in an isolated valley approximately one third of a mile from the village of Stoke Abbott, near Beaminster. The cottage was divided into two halves. John Hutchins, the owner, lived in one part with his wife and family, while a widower named James Seal lived in the other, with Sarah and her mother, Rebecca, as his lodgers. Although Sarah was illegitimate, she was 'of good and chaste character'. Unfortunately, twenty-three-year-old Sarah was also rather weak and sickly, with some deformities to her back and neck.

Since she was not a very robust young lady, she wasn't fit enough to work like the rest of her family and neighbours, who all laboured in the fields for local farmers. Therefore, on 30 April 1858, Sarah was at home alone, as she usually was, doing the housework and preparing supper.

In the middle of the afternoon, Jane Cornick, who was then more than seventy years old, walked down the lane to her garden, which was next to the cottage where Sarah spent most of her days by herself. While there, Jane Cornick heard a loud screech coming from Sarah's cottage. Knowing that Sarah would be alone, Jane scrambled up the bank surrounding her garden and peered over the hedge, calling Sarah's name several times as she did so.

She received no reply but as she watched, a young man called Jim Seal emerged from the door of Sarah's cottage. As he left the cottage, Seal ducked down as though he wanted to avoid being seen. However, as he crept away he spotted Jane Cornick standing on the bank, and turned to approach her.

Jane asked him what he had been up to to make Sarah scream – had he been 'making work' with her? Jim replied that he had been doing nothing of the sort, adding that he had left Sarah peeling potatoes for supper. Cornick noticed that his hands were bloody and that he had some blood on his trousers. She asked him what was wrong with his hands and was told that he had cut his finger on some grass. 'If grass would cut your hands, I should be cutting mine all day long, pulling up as much grass as I do', remarked Jane, giving him some paper from her pocket to wipe away the blood. She then walked with Jim for about 400 yards towards the village of Stoke Abbott before the two parted and went their separate ways. Jane went to visit her son but Jim Seal apparently had unfinished business with Sarah Guppy.

At about 4 p.m., people working nearby noticed smoke billowing from Buckshorn House and raised the alarm. On hearing that his home was on fire, James Seal ran from the fields. As soon as he entered the cottage, he saw Sarah lying on the floor with something covering her face. Shouting at her to get up and get out, Seal raced upstairs to try and save a few personal items from the flames. Only when he came downstairs again and saw Sarah still lying there did he realised that something was seriously wrong. With the help of his neighbours, he carried Sarah out to the small orchard adjoining the cottage and laid her on the grass. Once outside, in daylight, it was obvious that the poor girl's throat had been cut from ear to ear.

Meanwhile, Jane Cornick had heard about the fire and retraced her steps to Buckshorn House, arriving approximately three-quarters of an hour after she had previously left it in the company of Jim Seal. By that time, the cottage was almost completely destroyed by the fire, which had apparently started in an adjoining outbuilding. It seemed obvious that the killer of Sarah Guppy had deliberately set the fire in the hope that the evidence of his handiwork might be consumed in the flames.

The police were informed that a murder had been committed and PC William Lavender set out to investigate. However, by 5 p.m. he had got only as far as Horsehill when he was stopped by a local shepherd who told him that the man suspected of being the murderer had passed by only moments earlier. PC Lavender went after him and soon caught up with Jim Seal.

He noticed a bit of rag wrapped around Seal's right forefinger, covering a fresh wound. He also saw what looked like spots of blood on Jim's trousers. The bloodstains looked quite bright, although some had obviously been rubbed with dirt to disguise them. Jim also had blood on the right sleeve of his jacket, while the left sleeve had a large burn mark.

Lavender asked Jim how he had come by the cut on his finger and was told that he had gashed it with a knife while trying to cut a stick at nearby Bowood. When Lavender asked where the knife was, Jim explained that he had borrowed it from a carter and then returned it. He claimed that he didn't know the carter's name, nor could he describe him, or even say how many horses he was driving. Next Lavender asked where the stick was but Jim told him that he had not actually cut one, since he had cut his finger.

Had Jim been anywhere near Buckshorn House that afternoon, asked Lavender. Jim swore that he had been to Honeycomb and Bowood to pick up some sticks, but he had no sticks with him at the time. Lavender warned him that, if he could not come up with a better explanation for the bloodstains on his clothing, then he would be arrested on a charge of murder. No better explanation was forthcoming and Jim Seal was duly taken into custody.

At the inquest into Sarah's death, the jury came to the conclusion that she 'was by Jim Seal feloniously, wilfully and with malice aforethought killed and murdered'. Seal was quickly brought before magistrates, who committed him for trial at the next Dorset Assizes.

At his trial Jim Seal changed his story. Now he maintained that he had been working at Broadwindsor on the day of the murder and had been paid for his labour with two quarts of cider. After drinking these, he claimed that he recalled very little. However, witnesses were called who remembered him working at Stoke Abbott on that day, less than a quarter of a mile from Sarah's home, and stated that when he left work there were no bloodstains on his clothes and no cut on his finger.

Noah Hussey, who lived next door to Jim Seal, testified to seeing Jim eating bread and cheese with a very pointed knife, similar in appearance to one of three found in the cottage, near to where Sarah's body had lain. Another witness, Mr Paul, told the court that he had watched Jim Seal rubbing yellowish dirt on his trousers at about 4.30 p.m. in a field on the afternoon of the murder.

The courtroom at Dorchester, 2008. (© R. Sly)

Jane Cornick gave evidence about what she had seen while visiting her garden on the day of the murder, telling the jury of hearing Sarah scream just once, in apparent terror, and telling the court, 'I fancied it was a sort of deathly scream'. When she left the cottage with Jim Seal there had been no signs of a fire, suggesting that Seal had returned and started the blaze in an effort to conceal the murder.

A key to the Hutchins's side of the cottage was found just outside the door to Sarah's home and it was widely known that Mrs Hutchins had given Sarah a key for safekeeping. Jim Seal had been a frequent visitor to the Hutchins's home, usually trying to scrounge money. However, shortly before the murder there had been an 'incident' and Mrs Hutchins had told Jim Seal never to come again. According to Rebecca Guppy, Seal had been hanging round making a nuisance of himself for some time and Sarah herself was of the opinion that he was up to no good.

In summing up the case for the jury, the judge told them that it was difficult to suggest a motive for the crime, but reminded them that many a crime had been committed in the past without an apparent motive. It was not their duty to speculate on a possible motive, rather they should look at the facts of the case and, if they believed that the proven facts tied the accused to the case, then they should find him guilty. If they had any doubts then they should acquit him, but if they were completely satisfied that Jim Seal had committed the crime then it was their duty to God and man to find him guilty.

The jury duly discharged their duty, finding Jim Seal guilty of the wilful murder of Sarah Ann Guppy. Seal did not look like a man capable of so diabolical an act, looking much younger than his twenty years and standing only a fraction over 5ft tall. However, appearances can be deceptive and, in this case, they obviously were since Seal made a full confession just before his execution. He was hanged at Dorchester on 10 August 1858.

4

'IF YOU BIDE THERE CHAFING ME, I'LL GET UP AND BEAT THEE BRAINS OUT'

Preston, 1862

On 8 July 1862, former butcher John Cox of Preston near Dorchester received an important visitor. Cox, who lived in a small cottage with his elderly parents and two brothers, had for some time been suffering from a strange illness that manifested itself in fits and seizures that left him unable to work.

During the previous November, Cox had served a short prison sentence for poaching. In a routine check of the cells one morning, a prison officer had found him lying motionless on his bunk, as if dead. His eyes were open and staring, his whole body was extremely cold and he would not, or could not, respond to any outside stimuli. The warder immediately sent for the prison surgeon, who professed himself baffled at Cox's condition. He could do nothing more than order that the prisoner should be closely observed and any sign of change reported to him immediately.

Cox lay in a catatonic state for two more days before awakening, at which point he became so violent that he had to be forcibly restrained by strapping him to his bed. By now the surgeon was of the opinion that Cox was suffering from catalepsy, which was causing mania; a state that he felt could recur at any time if Cox were stressed or annoyed.

Released from prison into the care of his parents, Cox's condition worsened steadily as the months passed. His speech was rambling and by the following summer, according to the parish rector, Revd Baker, he was in such a state of confusion that it was impossible

Preston village at the turn of the nineteenth century.

even to pray with him. Cox apparently believed that he was hearing the voice of God and that God was telling him that He had come to take him.

One can only imagine the distress of Cox's elderly parents, confined for twenty-four hours a day in a tiny two-roomed cottage with someone who was no longer the son they had once loved, but a violent, unstable and highly dangerous man. Richard and Mary Cox were terrified of their son, to the extent that Richard had buried razors and other sharp implements from his home under the cabbages in his garden to prevent John from finding and using them against him. In an effort to help John, his parents called in Dr Adam Stapleton Puckett, the surgeon at the nearest Union Workhouse. Puckett, who was then sixty-five, lived in nearby Broadwey with his disabled wife and three grown-up children. Having diagnosed John Cox as suffering from 'brain fever', Puckett made several visits to see him over a period of three weeks, frequently in the company of the Revd Baker. Cox grew to hate the doctor, whom he was convinced was feeding him 'poison stuff'.

By 8 July, Puckett had exhausted every avenue of treatment and felt that, in the interests of everyone's safety, it would be best to remove John Cox to the Union. It must be remembered that in those days the prospect of entering the Union Workhouse was universally viewed with great trepidation, the ultimate in shame and degradation and the lowest point to which a person's circumstances could fall. Thus it was not expected that John Cox would agree willingly with the surgeon's decision and, indeed, he had stated that he would sooner go to gaol than the workhouse. Nevertheless, Puckett was confident that he would be able to handle the violent and unpredictable man.

He arrived at Cox's cottage at about five o'clock in the afternoon, accompanied by Mr Zachariah White, the relieving officer of the Union. They were met outside by Richard Cox, who advised them not to go indoors as he believed it was far too dangerous. That very morning, Mr Cox explained, his son had stripped off all his clothes and rubbed his naked body with half a pound of butter, remaining unclothed until the afternoon. Puckett paid no heed to the old man's advice and, telling Mr Cox that he believed that he could pacify his son, he sent Mr White off to procure a horse and cart in which to transport Cox back to the Union. The expected confrontation drew a cluster of curious onlookers from the village, who collected outside John Cox's bedroom window in order to obtain the best possible view of the proceedings.

On entering the cottage, Puckett found the illiterate Cox lying in bed pretending to read a book, dressed only in a flannel nightshirt. He politely asked Cox to get up so that he could help him to get dressed then take him outside for some air.

Cox responded angrily, 'If you bide there chafing me, I'll get up and beat thee brains out.'

Puckett responded in kind, telling Cox that if he struck him, then he would strike him back.

'Yes, I should like to have a turn with you', replied Cox, suddenly leaping out of bed and rushing at the doctor. His behaviour at this point was so terrifying that the crowd of onlookers hurriedly retreated from outside the bedroom window, shutting themselves in a nearby cottage and watching the rest of the proceedings through a window in relative safety. Sensing trouble, Richard Cox went to the village blacksmith to summon assistance

Neighbours saw Puckett rush out of the cottage and slam the door behind him, holding it tightly closed with one hand while brandishing a pair of fire tongs in the other. Next, they saw Cox break his bedroom window with part of a bedpost. This seemed to alarm Puckett, as he let go of the door and ran off up the garden as fast as his legs could carry him. Seconds later, Cox burst through the cottage door and set off in pursuit, a large piece of broken bedpost clutched in each hand.

He soon caught up with Puckett and began to belabour him with the bedposts until Puckett fell to the ground, bloody and bruised. Apparently satisfied with his work, Cox went to the window of one of the nearby cottages and asked for some brandy, threatening to kill the occupants if he didn't get it. He had three people to kill, he told them and he had already killed one of them.

He was given a tot of brandy, after which he returned to his cottage and put on a white shirt, neglecting to put on any clothes from the waist down. When he emerged, he was carrying a large saw. By now his father was back from the blacksmith's and asked John what he had been doing. Picking up a large stone as if to throw it at his father, John threatened the old man that he would kill him too if he didn't leave. Wisely, Richard Cox retreated to the lane outside his cottage, where he waited to try and forestall Mr White on his return.

As the villagers watched in horror, John Cox then approached the body of Mr Puckett and began to dismember it. He slowly and deliberately sawed off the head, throwing it into the road. He then removed one of the hands and similarly discarded that, followed

Adam Puckett's grave at Broadwey, 2008. (© N. Sly)

by one of Puckett's feet. Seeming to tire, he then walked back into his cottage before appearing a little while later, still trouser-less, carrying a bag. He set off across the fields towards the village of Osmington.

There he met Mr Joseph Townsend working in his garden. Cox called out to Townsend, whom he knew, asking him to come with him and not let anyone hurt him. In view of Cox's state of undress, Townsend first decided to get him decently attired and took him into the stable of the Plough Inn. The alarm had been raised in Preston as soon as Cox had left the village and the police had immediately alerted Richard Bartlett, the Osmington constable, who caught up with Cox in the stable just as he was recounting in gruesome detail to Townsend exactly what he had done and why he had left Preston so hurriedly, without having taken the necessary time to dress himself properly.

Cox was indicted for the wilful murder of the Union surgeon and stood trial just two weeks later before Mr Justice Keating at the Assizes in Dorchester. He was appointed a defence counsel, Mr Turner, who predictably argued that Cox was in such a state of mind at the time of the killing that he was not responsible for his conduct, being mentally incapable of distinguishing between right and wrong.

The jury acquitted John Cox of the murder of Adam Stapleton Puckett, finding him not guilty on the grounds of insanity. He was ordered to be detained in safe custody during Her Majesty's pleasure. His destination after the trial – presumably Dorchester Prison – is not recorded, although the whereabouts of Mr Puckett are easier to trace. He is buried in the churchyard at Broadwey, with a headstone that reads:

Sacred to the memory of
ADAM STAPLETON PUCKETT
who was murdered by a patient while
in the execution of his duty at
Sutton Pointz on the 8th day of July 1862,
in the 65th year of his age.
He was highly respected and deeply lamented
by all who knew him and was upwards
of twenty years Parochial medical officer
of the Upwey and Chickerell district.
Also of ELIZABETH ESTHER, relict of the
above who died January 6th 1865,
aged 66 years.
The Lord gave and the Lord hath taken away.

5

'SEE WHAT COMES OF ANNOYING A NERVOUS MAN'

Walditch, 1862

Daniel Joseph Stone and Charles Fooks were neighbours, living about thirty yards apart in the village of Walditch near Bridport. They were also first cousins and for many years had nurtured a disagreement between them, the origins of which were long forgotten. Family members and neighbours had made countless attempts to patch up the simmering quarrel between the two men and persuade them to shake hands but had never succeeded, mainly because Fooks seemed to be completely paranoid about his cousin and was convinced that Stone was spying on him, laughing at him and spreading rumours behind his back in order to blacken his character and drive him from the village.

Matters came to a head at about eight o'clock on the morning of 29 August 1862. Fooks was standing by the open door of his farmhouse with his gun in his hand. The door of his house opened directly onto the street and, as Fooks watched, he saw Stone walking along the road towards him.

It seemed as if the opportunity to finally rid himself of his long-time enemy was too good a one to miss and, as Stone passed the house, Fooks raised the gun to his shoulder, took careful aim at the back of Stone's head and fired. Stone instantly fell to the ground while Fooks calmly turned and went back inside, closing the door behind him. Moments later a second gunshot was heard from within the house.

Neighbours rushed to Stone's assistance but the gunshot wounds to the back of his head were so severe that, even as they reached him, he was already drawing his last gasping breaths. With Stone beyond all help, the neighbours turned their attention to Fooks.

The door to his house was firmly locked and no amount of knocking or shouting elicited any response from within. Eventually, a villager climbed to the first-floor window and saw Fooks lying on the floor, apparently dead. The front door was then broken open and, on closer examination, it was found that Fooks was merely wounded. He was still conscious and able to speak. A shotgun lay close by, and one barrel had recently been discharged. The other barrel appeared to be still loaded, but with gunpowder only.

The police and a doctor were sent for. Mr Hay, a local surgeon, examined Fooks and found him to have large but superficial wounds to his lips, left eyebrow and scalp. All were blackened, as if caused by a gun fired at very close range. Given that one barrel of the gun was still loaded with powder only, the doctor was unable to determine whether Fooks had genuinely attempted to kill himself or whether he had just loaded the recently-fired barrel with powder only and pretended to commit suicide. The doctor described Fooks as being 'excited' although he calmed down within a few minutes and his pulse, which had hitherto been quick but weak, returned to its normal steady beat.

Fooks was interviewed by the police and given the usual cautions. However, in spite of this he was unable to contain himself and expressed some pleasure on learning of Stone's death, saying that Stone had been teasing him and slandering him for months and that he had long wished him dead. 'See what comes of annoying a nervous man', he told the inspector.

Although Fooks was a respectable man, holding the positions of parish overseer and way-warden in the village of Walditch, he seemed to have a long history of mental and physical illness. He had frequently complained about pains in his head, which he believed were caused by some disease in his chest. He constantly experienced a burning sensation there, which his doctor had diagnosed as indigestion. A year or so before the murder, Fooks had told his doctor that he felt that the devil was within him and had asked for some strong medicine to drive it out. He had complained of feeling low and fit for nothing and of experiencing all sorts of 'queer feelings' and had been thinking of drowning himself. He was 'all confusion' and 'couldn't settle to anything'. When his doctor reminded him that he had much to be thankful for, he had agreed and told the doctor that he believed that some strong medicine would soon set him right.

Fooks was committed for trial at the Spring Assizes at Dorchester before Mr Serjeant Shee. Mr Collier and Mr Prideaux prosecuted, while Mr Coleridge and Mr Stock handled Fooks's defence.

The crux of the defence was that Fooks was insane and at the time of the murder had been completely delusional, believing that Stone was constantly laughing and jeering at him and was also slandering him to other people in an attempt to discredit him.

Several Walditch villagers testified at the trial to the effect that Fooks was often heard threatening to shoot people, Stone in particular. He had apparently stated several times that shooting people meant no more to him than shooting a rook or a stray cat and, when asked if he knew what the consequences of shooting someone would be, had replied that perhaps he should shoot himself.

Martha Hallett, Fook's niece, had lived with her bachelor uncle for fifteen years, leaving his home the day before the murder because, she claimed, she had come to fear him.

She told the court that for the past eight years Fooks had suffered from nervousness and unbearable pains in the head, which he had treated himself with repeated applications of vinegar. His bedroom was kept almost sealed, with blankets and carpets hung at the windows to prevent air entering, contrary to the advice of his doctor who believed that fresh air would be beneficial to him.

In the years that she had lived with her uncle, Martha had heard him threaten to kill himself numerous times. He was very fond of shooting and had been known to shoot out of his front door in the past. She had even heard him threaten to shoot Stone if he ever walked past the farmhouse.

Fooks had banned Martha from speaking to Daniel Stone and, although she had respected his request, he had still frequently accused her of secretly conversing with Stone. Another niece, Jane Fooks, stated that while her uncle was always kind to her, she had noticed him becoming more and more nervous over the last few months.

Villager Stephen Hawker had met Fooks shortly before the shooting and testified that Fooks had complained to him that he 'barely knew what he was about' and was struggling to control his temper. Both of Fooks's nieces spoke of the 'fits of passion' that Fooks flew into if anyone upset him and, at such times, he would wildly threaten to shoot anyone and everyone.

On the evidence of those who had known Fooks for many years, it certainly appeared as if a diagnosis of insanity would be an appropriate one. However, doctors who had seen him in prison since the murder seemed to disagree among themselves as to the extent of Fook's insanity.

Dr Harrington-Tuke, who saw Fooks in prison, had introduced himself to the accused as a 'mind doctor' but stated that Fooks had not been particularly interested in him, paying more attention to the prison doctor who was in the room at the time. Fooks had received Harrington-Tuke as if he had just arrived for a pleasant morning visit. The doctor had said that Fooks looked well, to which he replied that he was far from well, having pains in his head and stomach.

The murder was freely discussed, with Fooks commenting to the doctor that he would never have believed he could have hurt anybody. Asked if Stone had ever done anything to hurt him, he had hesitated before replying, 'No, not exactly.' He then went on to elaborate that his main grievance with Stone was that the man was always mocking him and scoffing at him and that he had spread reports intended to take away Fooks's character.

Asked by the doctor to name a specific incident, Fooks again struggled to recall one. Eventually, he remembered an occasion when an acre of his fields had been planted with docks, something he suspected Stone of having done. Asked if this was the reason why he had shot Stone, Fooks said that it wasn't and again stated that the reason for the shooting was that Stone was taking away his character.

'Were you insane at the time?' asked the doctor.

'Oh no, no sir, I'm not mad', replied Fooks, although he admitted to feeling 'in a daze' just before he had fired the fatal shot.

It was Harrington-Tuke's opinion that Fooks was of unsound mind and that he possessed homicidal and suicidal tendencies that could surface at any time, but especially if he were under stress. The effects of these tendencies were to negate any self-control in the prisoner, thus making him not responsible for his actions.

When it was pointed out to Harrington-Tuke in court that Fooks had had access to weapons for many years but had never before attempted to kill anyone, the doctor tried to explain himself in simpler terms, stating that he did not believe that Fooks had homicidal mania, but an ordinary mania with occasional homicidal tendencies. When he raised the gun to shoot Stone, he was well aware that the gun could – and probably would – kill him, but was incapable of resisting the urge to fire.

Asked if he was, as a man of science, prepared to swear on oath that at the time Fooks raised the gun he didn't know that what he was doing was wrong, Harrington-Tuke baulked at going quite that far. Telling the court that he had the greatest difficulty in answering that question, all he was prepared to say was that Fooks now knew that what he had done was wrong but at the time of the murder was acting on an uncontrollable impulse.

The final witnesses to appear were Dr Good, the prison surgeon, and his deputy, Mr Kyme. Good testified that he had seen and spoken to Fooks almost every day of his incarceration. He had seen no indications whatsoever to make him suspect that Fooks was insane. He was not incoherent, was not suffering from delusions and appeared perfectly rational at all times.

Mr Kyme gave exactly the same evidence, adding that the prisoner was always quiet and never appeared excited in any way. He was attended at all times by two warders, but only because he had attempted suicide before being admitted to prison. Since his imprisonment, he had shown neither homicidal nor suicidal tendencies.

Both Good and Kyme stated in court that they had not expected the defence to be one of insanity and had therefore not made any particular study of the prisoner's mind, nor sought any expert opinions, basing their testimony on common sense and previous practice rather than on reading. They were convinced that Fooks was completely sane, both now and at the time of the murder.

Perhaps surprisingly, the jury chose to believe the two prison surgeons over all the other trial witnesses and returned a verdict of 'Guilty'. Charles Fooks, aged forty-nine, was hanged at Dorchester on 27 March 1863.

Today, with our advanced medical knowledge, it seems reasonable to suggest that Fooks may have been suffering from schizophrenia, since he appears to have displayed many of the characteristic symptoms including paranoia, delusions, depression, confusion, suicidal tendencies, poor concentration and mood swings. He was, as suggested by his defence counsel, just as much or more the object of pity as Stone and was entitled, at the hands of the jury, to 'that protection which the law of England gave and was bound to give to persons whom it had pleased God to visit with the calamity of insanity'.

[Note: The name Fooks is alternatively spelled Fookes in some contemporary accounts of the murder.]

6

'I DID THE ACT, BUT NOT INTENTIONALLY, SIR'

Portland Convict Prison, 1863–1870

Life had not been kind to Edwin Alfred Preedy. An illegitimate baby, he had moved to London from Warwickshire while still an infant with his mother, Ann, and his aunt, Mary Smith. At four years old he fell downstairs, crashing heavily from top to bottom and colliding head first with a heavy wooden stool. His concerned mother and aunt rushed to see if he was all right, finding him lying unconscious, with blood pouring from his nose and mouth.

Edwin's aunt wanted to call a doctor but his mother pointed out that doctors cost money and they had none. Little Edwin was carried gently back upstairs to his bed, where he was devotedly nursed back to health by his mother and aunt. He was ill for a long time and, even after he had recovered, was never the same cheerful little boy that he had been before the fall. He was nervous and edgy during the day, but his real problems started at nightfall, when he was terrified of being left alone in the dark.

Such was his terror that his mother felt she had no option but to allow the little boy to sleep with her. This arrangement continued until Edwin's mother met and married Bill Edwards. A printer by trade, Edwards was a steady man of good character, but he had one blind spot – Edwin. Edwards complained that Ann was making the boy soft and refused to allow her to comfort Edwin at night. Bill Edwards had his own way of dealing with his stepson's problems and determined to beat the boy's fears out of him, not just with spankings, but by thrashing him over and over again with a heavy cane topped with a metal knob.

Edwin was humiliated at school, being teased cruelly by the other children about his 'difference'. In the evenings all he had to look forward to were long, dark, terrifying nights and savage beatings. Bill Edwards was not afraid to vent his wrath on Edwin's mother if she tried to intervene, so the poor woman felt she had no choice but to stand by and watch her son being brutalised. When Edwin's aunt saw wounds on his head and threatened to have a word with 'that brute' Bill Edwards, the new Mrs Edwards was petrified and begged her not to interfere, saying that she would be beaten if anything were said.

Edwin eventually reached the end of his tether at the age of thirteen and ran away from home. For a while he lived rough with a group of other homeless boys, until he was picked up one night and taken to St Giles Workhouse in the West End of London.

When he arrived at the workhouse, Preedy fought desperately to escape, kicking, screaming, biting, foaming at the mouth and growling like an animal. The workhouse doctor diagnosed typhus fever and Edwin was nursed until he recovered. So wild was the boy that, for the most part of his stay, he was tied to his bed, only being released to eat and be washed.

As he recovered, Edwin gradually calmed down until, by the time his physical illness was cured, he was transformed from a raging maniac to a pleasant and likeable boy. The workhouse had managed to establish his identity and, once he was fully fit, released him back into the care of his mother and stepfather. Now too old for school, Edwin was given a job with Bill Edwards and began to learn the printer's trade. However, now he was with the boy all day, Edwards grew ever more vicious and sadistic in his treatment of him. Edwin Preedy seemed to develop a dual personality – normally a charming and engaging young man, when beaten or abused he turned into a raging animal, behaving like a madman.

He soon tired of Edwards's cruelty towards him and ran away from home again, this time forsaking London altogether for the Warwickshire countryside of his birth. Part of his motive for heading to Warwickshire was a desire to find his real father, but, before he had much of a chance to start looking, he was arrested on a charge of larceny and served an eight-month prison sentence in Warwick Castle.

On his release from prison, Preedy signed up for the Army, serving with the 85th Regiment of Foot. He was quickly promoted to Corporal and then promptly deserted. Turning to crime as the only real way to support himself, Preedy was soon arrested and sentenced to serve ten weeks in Carmarthen Prison. There it was discovered that he was a deserter and, understandably, the Army wanted him back so that they could punish him for his crime.

When given this news by the prison governor, Preedy instantly erupted into a maelstrom of violence. 'I'll swing for you bastards rather than go back in the Army!' he screamed. Wildly swinging his prison issue wooden clogs he began to belabour the warders who had escorted him to the governor's office. He overturned the governor's desk onto the legs of two warders he had knocked to the floor and, as more and more warders came rushing from other parts of the prison, he kept them at bay by clubbing them with chairs.

A cell at Portland Prison.

It took several officers to overpower him and, when the Army claimed him, the escorting officers had to keep him shackled hand and foot. He was subjected to a disciplinary hearing in Pembrokeshire, where he was dishonourably discharged and sent on his way. Soon afterwards he was arrested for stealing some clothes and given a three-year prison sentence, to be served at Haverfordwest.

Finding Preedy too much of a handful, the Welsh authorities had him transferred to Milbank Prison in London, where he attacked and injured a warder in one of his rages, receiving a flogging as a result. Memories of his ill treatment at the hands of his stepfather came flooding back and, from that moment on, his behaviour became more and more crazed until it was decided that there was only one place for him – Portland Convict Prison, the toughest prison in England.

On 8 September 1862, three prisoners – Thomas Moore, John Ashton and James Schofield – walked along the landing of Portland Prison. Under the supervision of warder Charles Evans, it was their job to collect from each prisoner the empty food tin that had contained his supper and the knife with which he had been issued in order to eat it. As they opened the door to Cell 727, Preedy was standing waiting to pass over his cutlery. As Moore approached him to take the utensils, at the very last minute Preedy dropped the tin and, still holding the knife, pushed past Moore onto the landing. Before any of the men could react, Preedy seized Warder Evans from behind and stabbed him in the throat, twisting the knife violently.

Moore and Ashton each grabbed one of Preedy's arms while Schofield set off to fetch help. As soon as he was released from Preedy's grasp, Evans reflexively staggered a few steps before dropping to the floor, dead.

Portland Convict Prison, late 1800s.

Reinforcements arrived in the form of Warder Thomas Roberts, who quickly assessed the scene then drew his cutlass and hit Preedy over the head with the flat of the blade, rendering him unconscious. By the time Preedy came round again, he was safely shackled.

Asked why he had stabbed Evans, Preedy maintained that there was something between the two men. Saying that he was glad that Evans was dead, Preedy explained that he had eaten his supper, read his Bible and then decided to kill Evans.

Preedy received a visit from prison chaplain, Mr Duke, but that was enough to send him into another rage. As soon as Duke had left the cell, Preedy was once more calm and polite, explaining to Warder James Douglas that he was a Catholic.

The task of moving Preedy to Dorchester Prison fell to Superintendent Underwood of the Dorset Police. Approaching the job with trepidation, Underwood was pleasantly surprised to find Preedy calm and compliant and expressing remorse for killing Warder Evans, having since been told that Evans was a married man with several children. Preedy confessed that there was nothing personal between him and his victim. People had been picking on him and he had simply made up his mind to kill the first warder that came along.

Preedy's apparent complacency lulled warders at Dorchester Prison into a false sense of security. Placed in solitary confinement, he ranted, raved and tried to injure himself, having to be kept naked as he immediately destroyed any clothing he was issued with. The prison governor, Mr J.V.D. Lawrence, knew that being kept in solitary confinement was what was upsetting Edwin, but did not dare move him in with other prisoners for fear of him killing someone.

Edwin Preedy behaved like a madman for the first month of his stay in Dorchester, but eventually calmed down and became a model prisoner. He took to nursing injured birds back to health and was absolutely heartbroken when he accidentally stepped on one of his 'patients' and killed it.

Preedy's mild-mannered behaviour lasted until his trial at Dorchester Assizes before Judge Sergeant Shea. As the trial opened, Preedy was asked whether he pleaded guilty or not guilty, to which he responded, 'I did the act, but not intentionally, sir'. When told he must either say 'Guilty' or 'Not Guilty', after apparently giving the matter some thought, he chose the latter.

Before long, he violently objected to evidence given by Thomas Moore and tried to vault over the edge of the dock to get to him. As guards did their best to hold him, he rained blows on them. It took ten men to finally subdue him, then, with his arms pinioned by his sides, the court watched in astonishment as Preedy, in an attempt to choke himself, managed somehow to throw his own head back so far that he was able to bite a piece of the cloth from the back of his own jacket. When the guards restrained him even tighter, he then tried to bite pieces from the wooden edge of the dock.

Mr Good, the prison surgeon, tried to calm him. By now Preedy was all smiles again, offering to shake hands with the surgeon. When Good declined, Preedy once more flew into a tantrum.

Eventually the judge could take no more. After asking Good if he thought Preedy fit to stand trial and receiving an affirmative reply, he turned to Preedy and offered him a ten-minute break to compose himself. When Preedy didn't respond, the clerk of the court, Mr Corne, repeated the question to him, prompting a rambling discussion from the prisoner about how and where he knew Corne. Saying that Corne was a man that he could trust and offering to shake hands with him, Preedy refused to acknowledge anybody in court but Corne, cursing and shouting if Mr Good tried to approach him.

Reluctantly, Judge Shea informed the court that he was perfectly satisfied that Preedy was sane, but, for everyone's safety, Preedy must be restrained before proceedings could continue. Two broad leather belts were fetched and used to strap Preedy's legs together and to pin his arms to his sides. However, before Shea could pick up the trial where he had left off, Preedy tensed his muscles and both belts snapped with loud cracks. Warders just managed to grab him before he leapt from the dock.

Shea stormed out of the court to consult with a colleague, Mr Justice Byles, returning some time later having given orders that Preedy was to be shackled in chains. This done, Preedy alternately fought against his bindings and slumped exhausted in the dock, appearing to sleep. The judge eventually adjourned the trial for a short period of consultation with Mr Good, local doctor Alfred Emson and the surgeon from Portland Prison, William Houghton. Finding himself seriously doubting Preedy's sanity, Shea sought the opinions of the three medical men as to whether or not the prisoner was fit to stand trial. Having been assured by all three doctors that he was, Shea resumed the trial.

Among those giving evidence at the trial were Preedy's mother, who testified to his fall downstairs, his strangeness in childhood and the terrible beatings he had received at the hands of his stepfather. At one point Ann Preedy fainted and, trying vainly to reach her, Preedy fell sideways off his chair in a crash of chains.

By the time the jury had retired for about half an hour and returned with a verdict of 'guilty of wilful murder' against Preedy, the accused was once again docile and calm enough to hear the judge pronounce the death sentence upon him.

In doing so the judge told Preedy that at least he would have time to make his peace with the Almighty God, a privilege that had been denied his victim and, after the trial, Edwin Preedy spent a lot of time in the company of the Revd H. Moule, the vicar of Fordington. Moule was not a priest, but it didn't matter because Preedy was not a Catholic. When a kindly, well-meaning Catholic from Chideock tried to arrange a prison visit from a priest for him, Preedy sent him a message saying that he was not, had never been, and would never be a Catholic.

Through Moule, Preedy made a full confession, adding that to be executed was a just punishment for a sinner such as he. He admitted to feigning madness at his trial in the hope of avoiding the death sentence. When asked why he hadn't just punched Evans rather than stabbed him, Preedy pointed out that the last time he had tried punching someone he had been flogged.

As the date of his execution approached, Preedy asked Moule to procure several small Bibles for him. He then inscribed each one personally and presented one to all the prison warders to whom he had been abusive. He also spent time making bead rings, one of which he was to give to executioner Calcraft as he mounted the scaffold.

On 27 March 1863, twenty-year-old Preedy stood at the scaffold in the company of Charles Fooks (see Chapter 5). Preedy was calm and contrite, wanting to shake hands with the prison governor and the under-sheriff and was visibly hurt when they snubbed him. A crowd of almost 5,000 people watched as Preedy took the drop, not

Portland Borstal Institution, 1930s.

Convicts going to work at the stone quarries, Portland Prison, 1917.

dying instantly but instead kicking and convulsing violently for some time before finally becoming still. After hanging for an hour, the two bodies were cut down and buried within the confines of the prison walls.

AFTERWORD

Historically, the regime in Portland Prison was harsh and brutal. Opened in 1848, the death rate amongst inmates was unusually high, and suicides and attempted suicides were commonplace. During the 1870s an average of one inmate died every week. Preedy's fatal attack on Warder Charles Evans is just one of several fatalities recorded among both guards and prisoners.

On 23 March 1869, Jonah Dethridge, a native of Wednesbury, killed Assistant Warder Jospeh Trevett by striking him over the head with a steel-tipped pick. About three weeks previously, Trevett had reported Dethridge for insolence and Dethridge had been punished. On the morning of the murder, Dethridge, who was serving a seven-year sentence for theft, was one of a party of sixteen convicts engaged in building fortifications to the Verne Citadel, an Army barracks and prison on the Isle of Portland. Trevett reproached him about his work, to which Dethridge responded with a stream of bad language, saying that he would 'work how he damned well wanted.'

About an hour later, Trevett was standing on an embankment, when Dethridge was seen to creep up behind him. Before anyone could stop him, he swung his pickaxe and

Convict quarries at Portland Prison, 1908.

dealt Trevett a heavy blow to his head. Trevett was known as a humane and kind officer and the other convicts were quick to go to his defence. However, before they could reach him, Trevett toppled forward from the embankment and Dethrridge jumped down after him and hit him twice more.

Trevett's skull was fractured and he died in hospital later the same day. Dethridge was tried at the Dorset Assizes before Mr Justice Lush on 22 July 1869. Known as being both sullen and insolent, Dethridge showed little emotion throughout his trial, even smiling as he was found guilty and sentenced to death.

He remained indifferent to his fate in the run-up to his execution on 12 August 1869, refusing to allow anyone to pray for his soul as he mounted the scaffold at Dorchester, where he reluctantly agreed to shake hands with Calcraft, his executioner. His death was instantaneous and, like Preedy, he was subsequently buried within the prison walls. Trevett was buried in the graveyard of St George's Church in Portland, where his headstone simply records that he was 'murdered by a convict in 1869'.

Less than one year later, Assistant Warder Edward Love Bly met his death at the hands of prisoner Thomas Ratcliffe. Bly was in charge of a work party of seventeen convicts on 20 April 1870, also working on the fortifications. Like Dethridge before him, Ratcliffe had been reported and punished, and, on joining the gang that morning, had been heard to say that he intended to kill Officer Bly. Bly had been warned about this threat and had, as a consequence, tried to keep Ratcliffe out of reach of any tools that he might use as weapons. At about 2 p.m. Ratcliffe was given an order by Bly to move to a different part of the job, at which he picked up a shovel and moved towards Bly.

Another convict shouted out a timely warning and Bly was able to duck, so that the vicious blow aimed at his head instead caught his shoulder. Bly staggered away, but Ratcliffe followed, all the while raining blows with his shovel on any part of Bly that he could reach. One particular blow caught Bly on his shin, slicing through the flesh to the bone.

By the time other convicts had managed to subdue Ratcliffe and pin him to the ground, Bly was bleeding heavily. He managed to limp back to the prison, where he received treatment for numerous cuts and bruises, appearing to recover quickly from the assault. However, by 10 May it became evident that the wound on Bly's leg was becoming infected and he eventually died on 13 June from blood poisoning.

Ratcliffe was tried for killing Edward Bly at Dorchester in July 1870, before Mr Justice Willes. The main question at the trial was whether the charge against Ratcliffe should be one of murder or manslaughter. However, Ratcliffe rather sealed his own fate by testifying that, 'I did assault the officer. I tried to take his life and should have succeeded had not the other prisoners prevented me.'

Ratcliffe was found guilty of wilful murder and sentenced to death. Like Preedy and Dethridge before him, he was hanged by William Calcraft at Dorchester Prison on 15 August 1870.

Portland Prison was converted into a Borstal in 1921, and in 1965 an officer named Derek Lambert was killed by an inmate, who was later sentenced to life imprisonment for the murder. The prison became a Young Offenders Institution in 1988.

[Note: In various contemporary accounts of the murders of Portland Prison, the name of convict Thomas Moore is also recorded as John Moore. Prison surgeon William Houghton is alternatively referred to as William Hawler. Joseph Trevett's surname is alternatively spelled Trevitt, while Thomas Ratcliffe's name is alternatively spelled Radcliffe.]

7

'I HOPE THEY WILL PROVE THAT I DID IT'

Hampreston, 1869

Twenty-four-year-old Emma Pitt had been a schoolmistress at the National School at Hampreston for several years. She was a respectable unmarried lady from a good family, who was described as being of the most excellent moral character. Normally Emma did not live on the school premises, instead boarding with her parents in neighbouring Wimborne Minster, although there was a bedroom and sitting room over the schoolrooms which she could use if she wanted.

By May 1869, tongues were wagging in and around Wimborne with the scandalous rumour that Miss Pitt was pregnant. Eventually one of the gossips, Esther Cook, could bear the suspense no longer and went directly to Emma to ask, 'Is it true what all the people are saying about you – that you are far gone in the family way?'

Emma was most indignant. Even though she was a slight, slender young woman and her condition was obviously visible, she categorically denied being pregnant and accused the villagers of lying and trying to blacken her character. However, just weeks later, on 15 June, she arrived at the school in the morning and, instead of going to her classroom as normal, went straight upstairs to the bedroom, saying that she felt unwell.

A neighbour of the school, Mrs Elizabeth Parsons, firmly believed that Emma was pregnant, thinking her to be about six months into her term. Hearing that morning that she was ill, she went upstairs to check on her and realised immediately that not only was Emma definitely pregnant, but she was actually about to give birth. Knowing Emma's prickly reaction to any suggestion that she might be expecting a baby, Mrs Parsons said nothing to her on the subject, although she did suggest that the school children were given a half-holiday and sent home. Emma wouldn't hear of it, knowing that any such action would only serve to fuel the gossips. Hence the students were left in the charge of a pupil-teacher, Miss Julia Guy, and, after fetching Emma a cup of tea with a tot of brandy in it, Mrs Parsons went home. She checked on Emma several more times during the day, giving her more tea and brandy. Each time, Emma maintained that her illness was nothing more than a violent attack of sickness and diarrhoea. She asked Mrs Parsons for some ginger, saying that she was suffering from wind and also told her that she had taken gin and some tincture of rhubarb, but had been unable to keep them down.

Mrs Parsons returned at about half past three in the afternoon to find Emma still in labour – and still vehemently denying the fact that she was pregnant.

After the school day had finished at four o'clock and the children had all gone home, Miss Guy herself went upstairs to check on Emma, who begged her not to let Mrs Parsons come near her again. Accordingly, when Miss Guy left the building shortly afterwards, she made sure that the front door of the school was locked behind her.

Mrs Parsons came back at about five o'clock and, having tried the front door and found it locked against her, simply walked round the building to the back door. As she entered the school she was met by Emma Pitt walking down the stairs.

Emma seemed quite put out at seeing her neighbour, asking her how she had managed to get in. Still obviously unwell and very weak, she made no protest when Mrs Parsons announced her intention of procuring a cart so that Emma could be driven home. As Mrs Parsons helped Emma into the cart, she noticed that the front of her dress was bloodstained.

It was now obvious to Mrs Parsons that Emma was no longer pregnant. As soon as she had sent Emma on her way, she rushed straight upstairs to the school bedroom, accompanied by her daughter, Sarah Newman. Noticing some bloodstains on the bedding and the bedroom floor, they began a frantic search for the baby, which they eventually found concealed in a drawer beneath a patchwork quilt. The child – a boy – was dead, although still warm. He lay on his back, heavily bloodstained, his mouth wide open. His head was very bruised and the umbilical cord had been roughly torn several inches from his body.

Mrs Parsons immediately sent for the police. The first officers to arrive were Deputy Chief Constable John Hammond and Constable Adams, who also noted the large amount of blood on the bedroom floor and the bed linen. The body of the infant was taken to the police station and placed in a locked cell until the surgeon could examine it. Meanwhile, Hammond went straight to Miss Pitt's home and arrested her. He described her as talking rationally and of being capable of understanding what was said to her, although in a much weakened physical state.

However, later that evening she was examined by a doctor, who found her to be in a very excited state and talking incoherently. There was no doubt in the doctor's mind that she had recently been confined. A female superintendent was brought in to take care of her and it was not until 2 July that Emma had recovered sufficiently to be formally charged with the wilful murder of her baby. Her only comment was, 'I hope they will prove that I did it'.

On the day after the baby's birth, the school bedroom was searched again In the same drawer where the infant's body had been found was the child's tongue, cut from his mouth and wrapped in a piece of rag, which had then been tied up with a blue ribbon. A large stone, usually used to prop open the bedroom door, was found on the stairs leading to the bedroom, heavily stained with blood.

When the body of the baby was examined, it was discovered that the child's jaw had been broken in five places and his tongue clumsily removed with some kind of sharp instrument. Dr Druitt, the surgeon, likened the severity of the damage to the child's mouth to that which he would normally have expected to see from a shotgun wound. There was a deep cut on the side of the baby's mouth and severe bruising on its forehead. Druitt believed that the baby was full term and had not been stillborn. He determined the cause of the infant's death as suffocation due to congealed blood in the throat.

Emma Pitt stood trial for the wilful murder of her baby boy at the Summer Assizes in Dorchester on 23 July 1869, pleading 'Not Guilty'. Mr Justice Lush presided, with Mr Ffooks and Mr Nugent Bankes prosecuting, and Mr Collins acting for the defence. Because of the delicate nature of the case, the court was cleared of women and children before the proceedings commenced.

The biggest question of the trial was whether or not the baby boy had ever had a separate existence to its mother. Two surgeons, Druitt and his assistant Mr Manning, were called to testify and it was their opinion that the wounds found on the child's body had been inflicted while the baby was alive, meaning that it had definitely existed as a separate entity from its mother. In spite of a vigorous cross-examination by the defence, during which Mr Collins cited studies made by eminent surgeons, both of the medical witnesses stuck firmly to their opinions. Collins asked whether they had removed the child's lungs to see if they would float in water, that being the test thought to prove conclusively whether or not the lungs had ever been inflated with air. Druitt maintained that he had not thought it necessary, since he believed that the bruising on the baby's forehead, the rigidity of its body when it was found and the retraction of the muscles around the cut on its mouth were sufficient proof that the child had lived and breathed independently.

At this point Mr Justice Lush addressed the jury and asked them whether or not they believed that the child had ever existed separately. If they did not believe that it had, then it would be futile to proceed with the trial.

The jury debated for a few minutes before informing the judge that they would like to hear the case out.

Mr Collins then argued strenuously for his client, telling the jury that the only evidence against his client was the opinion of the medical men, which he summarised as 'altogether a matter of conjecture'. There was, he told them, 'not a tittle of substantial evidence' on which they could rely.

Collins reminded them that no sharp instrument had ever been found, either in the bedroom or in Emma's possession, with which she might have removed her child's tongue and that although Emma's bedroom was directly above the schoolroom, no cry from a newborn infant had been heard. (He neglected to mention that the evidence heard in court seemed to suggest that Miss Guy and all the children had left the school by the time Emma Pitt had actually given birth!) Collins presented Emma Pitt as the pathetic victim of the unnamed man whose lust had destroyed her virtue rather than as a murderess. He pointed out that she would have suffered extreme bodily pain and shame at her condition and asked the jury to consider whether, if Emma had indeed murdered her baby, would she not have disposed of the body after doing so, rather than leaving it in the drawer as evidence of her guilt, which would inevitably lead to her detection?

Stressing that the charge against Emma Pitt was a capital charge, Collins implored the jury to think carefully before reaching their decision and to give her the benefit of any doubt that existed in their minds. They should remember that the life of a young girl was in their hands. Throughout Collins's address Emma Pitt sobbed piteously, her gaze fixed steadfastly on the jurors, as it had been throughout the trial.

After the defence counsel's speech, Mr Justice Lush then summed up the case for the jury. The crux of the matter, he told them, was whether or not the child had ever been an inhabitant of this world. If it had had a separate existence and its life had been extinguished as a result of an act by its mother, then the jury should find the accused guilty of wilful murder. Otherwise there was not the slightest doubt that Emma Pitt was guilty of the lesser offence of concealment of birth

The jury retired for only ten minutes before returning with a verdict of 'Not Guilty' of murder, but 'Guilty' of concealing the birth of a baby. Mr Justice Lush then addressed Emma, telling her that in his opinion this was one of the worst cases of concealment that had come before him. Her conduct during the day on which she was in labour, coupled with her constant denials of her situation to Mrs Parsons, proved conclusively what was her intention, at least with regard to concealment of the birth. For that reason he proposed to give her the maximum sentence allowed him by the law. Emma Pitt, whose face had visibly brightened at the jury's verdict of 'Not Guilty', once again burst into noisy sobs as she was sentenced to two years imprisonment with hard labour. She was escorted from the dock to be taken to prison, moaning and crying hysterically.

8

'I TRIED TO SETTLE ONE LAST LEAVE AND I HAVE SUCCEEDED THIS TIME'

Portland, 1891

The naval training ship HMS *Boscawen* first arrived in Portland in 1862, replacing HMS *Britannia*, which then moved from Portland to Dartmouth to become the forerunner of the Royal Naval College. The original *Boscawen* was replaced in 1873 by HMS *Trafalgar*, which subsequently adopted the name *Boscawen* and remained in Portland until 1906, when she was sold.

Life on a naval training ship in the nineteenth century was not easy for the boys on board, being taught the many and varied tasks they would have to do as men at sea. They learned the rudiments of reading and writing, along with how to set rigging, use rifles, clean and maintain the ship, scrub and wash hammocks and make and mend clothes. They also took part in a punishing schedule of physical exercises and gymnastics. Fire being a great danger on a wooden ship at sea, the boys formed a fire brigade which, in emergencies, could be called on to assist with fires on land. On Sundays, every boy was expected to attend divine service. Discipline on the ship was harsh and in 1866 it is recorded that two boys each received twenty-four lashes from the birch.

By 1891 there were 549 boys on board the *Boscawen*, most aged between twelve and seventeen years old, with each boy receiving weekly pocket money of around 3*d*. As the boys were often prevented from leaving the ship for long periods, due to bad weather or

The Boscawen *training ship, 1905.*

an infectious illness, for which the entire ship was quarantined, life on *Boscawen* could be confining and claustrophobic.

On Sunday 15 November 1891, after attending the religious services, three of the *Boscawen* boys, William Groom, John Wise and Lawrence Salter, obtained permission to go ashore. Together they walked along the top of the cliffs at Portland towards Bow and Arrow Castle, enjoying a rare chance to stretch their legs, chatting and picking blackberries as they went.

William Groom was about thirty yards ahead of the other two, half listening to their conversation about the Shambles lightship, a vessel that warned other ships about the treacherous Shambles sandbar between Weymouth and Portland. Suddenly, what Groom later described as a 'groan' interrupted the talking, and then the conversation abruptly ceased altogether. Turning round to see what had happened, Groom saw John Wise perched precariously on the edge of the 100ft-high cliffs on his hands and knees, peering over the top and laughing loudly. Groom rushed to see what was going on and, as he looked over the cliff, he spotted 'a bundle of blue' at the bottom and realised that it was Lawrence Salter.

Children playing in the gardens of the nearby prison cottages had seen Salter fall and raised the alarm. A party of rescuers descended the cliffs, finding Salter still alive but terribly injured. He was brought carefully to the top and taken to the prison infirmary, where he died half an hour later.

Groom asked Wise if he had pushed Salter, but Wise made no reply, and just continued to laugh maniacally, so much so that his legs would no longer support him and he fell to the ground. By now, all the frightened Groom could think of was to get Wise back to the

Bow and Arrow Castle, Portland, 1917.

Boscawen. He seized Wise's hands, pulled him upright and began to walk him towards the ship. However, on their way back they met one of the ship's officers, Petty Officer First-Class Benjamin Stuckey, and, to his relief, Groom was able to hand Wise over into his charge, after telling the officer that he wished to report Wise because he believed that he had pushed Salter over the cliff. Wise immediately confessed to Stuckey that he had indeed done exactly that – he had deliberately pushed Salter over the cliff in order to get hanged.

Doubting that Wise could be in his right mind, Stuckey asked the boy if there was anything the matter with him, to which Wise replied that he was subject to 'fits of frenzy' and that he must have killed Salter in one of those fits.

Back on board the *Boscawen*, Wise repeated this statement to Lieutenant Andrew Stafford Mills, saying that he had gone ashore with the sole intention of killing somebody. 'I tried to settle one last leave and I have succeeded this time', he cheerfully told Mills, continuing to smile and laugh all the while he was being questioned.

An inquest was opened into the death of Lawrence Salter on 17 November, at the Grove Inn, Portland, before Coroner Sir Richard Howard. Wise smiled throughout, even as the coroner's jury recorded a verdict of wilful murder against him. At this, he was arrested and remanded in Dorchester Prison. Shortly afterwards he was brought before Mr Justice Cave at the Dorset Assizes, but the judge was not prepared to hear the case since the alleged murder had happened less than a week before and Wise had not yet been before magistrates. Describing Wise as a poor, friendless boy, Cave warned against pressing on with the case too hastily. In fairness, he said, Wise should be permitted to have witnesses for his defence and, since there were questions about his sanity, he also deserved the benefit of medical opinion.

John Wise duly appeared before magistrates at Dorchester on 11 December 1891. Mr Howard Bowen prosecuted the case and Wise was not defended. It was noted that he was in the hands of a medical expert who would give evidence at 'the proper time'. Wise was committed for trial at the next Assizes.

By the time the trial opened on 7 March 1892, before Mr Justice Wills at Dorchester, extensive investigations had been made into both his medical history and his current state of mind. Mr M.W. McKellar and Mr Evelyn Cecil prosecuted the case and Wise had by now been appointed a defence counsel, Mr A. Cardew.

The court heard accounts of the events of the day of the murder, followed by evidence from the master-at-arms of the *Boscawen*, Robert Franklin.

Franklin told the court that Salter, a native of West Ealing, London, had celebrated his sixteenth birthday the day before his death. He had joined the *Boscawen* on 16 September 1891 and was 'well conducted', as indeed was Wise.

Wise was sixteen-and-a-half years old at the time of Salter's death and had seven months service. During that time he had tried to commit suicide by swallowing oxalic acid. On 23 July 1891, he had boasted to his crewmates that, before joining the ship, he had strangled a young boy at Croydon and buried him behind the Roman Catholic school. When it was suggested that he was delusional, he had assured people that he wished he could think so, but sadly he knew it to be true. It was never established whether Wise's story was actually true or merely a figment of his fevered imagination. What was established, however, was that Wise was a very troubled young man.

Witnesses described him as being 'eccentric' ever since he was a child of eight years old, and his father and several other relatives had died in lunatic asylums. Although he had now changed his account of the events surrounding the death of Salter to say that the young sailor's death had been an accident, Wise had assured everyone prior to his trial that he had no personal grudge against his victim but had just seized the opportunity to kill him. There had been no scuffling or fighting, just one swift push. Wise had also said that he did not dislike being in the Navy but that he would just as soon be out of this world that in it.

The jury retired only briefly before returning with their verdict, finding John Wise guilty of the wilful murder of Lawrence Salter but stating that he was insane at the time of the killing. Ironically, for a boy who, by his own account, had committed murder specifically so that he might be hanged, Mr Justice Wills directed that Wise should be detained as a criminal lunatic in Dorchester Prison 'until her Majesty's pleasure should be known.'

9

'THIS IS ALL THROUGH MEN GOING TO MY HOUSE WHILE I'M AWAY'

Isle of Portland, 1902

Frank Burden was one of three brothers, originally from Gutch Common, Semley. Although Frank was close to his parents and his brothers, Ernest and Walter – so close that the boys were known locally as 'the triplets' – he had realised early on in life that the family farm was not large enough to support all of them comfortably. Hence, as soon as he was of age, Frank had prudently moved away from the area, first working as a carter for the biscuit-makers Huntley & Palmer at Reading, then taking up horticulture. He had lived a parsimonious life, carefully saving his money for the day when he would marry.

On 15 April 1899, his dreams came true when, at thirty-one years old, he married Emily Green. It was a strange union. Twenty-year-old Emily was a tall, rather beautiful young woman, while her husband was a thickset but small, almost dwarfish man, with a spinal deformity that twisted his back making him seem even smaller. He had un-shapely features and a sallow complexion, with an abnormally large nose, beneath which grew a luxuriant, black moustache. Nevertheless, in spite of his physical ugliness, he was a mild-mannered and good-natured man and his radiant bride seemed genuinely happy to be marrying him.

Only one thing threatened to mar the joy of the wedding celebrations. As Frank's brother Ernest came to congratulate his brother and wish him luck, he couldn't help but notice that Frank seemed strangely downhearted. When Ernest questioned him,

The Isle of Portland.

Frank admitted that his sadness came from knowing that his marriage would never be blessed with children. When Ernest told him that he couldn't possibly know that, Frank assured him that he knew for a fact that he was unable to father a child. Emily had not been told, said Frank, swearing his brother to secrecy and promising that he would tell her himself when he felt that the time was right.

Frank had secured a gardening job with a Mr Edward Pierce on the Isle of Portland and the newlyweds moved into rented rooms in Grove Street. Frank seemed somewhat ashamed of not being able to provide a house for his new wife, but Emily soon made their rooms comfortable and homely. However, Frank was an ambitious man who wanted to give her the best he possibly could and so, before long, the couple secured half a house on Reforne. Financially, renting half a house was still beyond their means, so the couple let out a room to a lodger, Jack Roberts. Before long, Ernest and Walter left the family farm and moved to Portland to be near their brother.

Frank and Emily lived happily together in their rented house, but their relationship was the subject of much gossip and innuendo in the small, tight-knit community. Unable to comprehend why a woman as beautiful as Emily would marry a man as ugly as Frank, people began to gossip behind her back, suggesting that she was enjoying an extra-marital relationship with the lodger.

The gossip eventually reached Frank's ears – as it was most probably intended to – and, although he didn't say anything to Emily, he reacted by giving Jack Roberts notice to leave his home and replacing him with his brother, Ernest. However, the gossip continued and now the alleged recipients of Emily's sexual favours were rent collector Abe Winter and

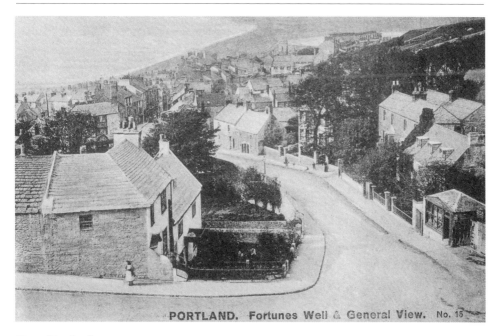

View of Portland.

his friend John Pearce. Frank brooded silently over the rumours, unable to talk to Emily about them, but inwardly seething with jealousy.

In January 1902 Emily announced to Frank that they were to have a baby. She was completely unprepared for her husband's reaction as he immediately rounded on her and angrily asked, 'What man have you been with?'

Stunned, Emily assured Frank that he was the only man she had slept with, telling him, 'This is your Emily you are talking to.'

'My Emily?' raged Frank. 'Ain't you Jack Roberts' Emily?'

The discussion turned into an argument, with Frank only now telling Emily the rumours he had heard about her supposed infidelity. When Ernest arrived home from work, Frank was still raging and his brother tried in vain to calm him down.

'Show me evidence that you can't father a child.' Ernest eventually demanded, when it was obvious that his efforts to placate Frank were not succeeding.

Frank had no answer. He continued to fume, announcing his intentions of coming home at unexpected times in the future and putting a ladder to his bedroom window in order to catch his wife 'at it'. Ernest eventually gave up trying to mediate and went to bed. Throughout the night he could hear the argument between his brother and sister-in-law continuing from their bedroom, although he was unaware that the verbal tirade had become a physical fight.

Eventually, pushed beyond her limits by her husband's irrationality, Emily landed a punch on his nose that immediately drew blood. Frank retaliated with a prolonged assault on his wife, although even in his extreme anger he was careful to confine his blows to areas that would be covered by her clothing.

The following morning Frank went to work as normal but, as he had told his brother, he made a surprise visit home in the afternoon. He found Emily in the company of her friend and former neighbour, Alice Scard. The two women were about to go for a walk and Frank expressed his surprise, reminding Emily that earlier that day she had told him that she could scarcely move for pain.

'Have you been unwell?' asked a concerned Mrs Scard, at which Emily promptly hitched up her skirts to show her neighbour the extensive bruising to her legs and hips which had resulted from Frank's savage beating.

Within days, Emily had written to her mother asking for money so that she could leave Frank. When a sovereign was sent, Emily told Mrs Scard that she was leaving.

As she packed her cases, Frank made another surprise visit home and quickly realised her intentions. Soon Mrs Scard was caught in the middle of a blazing row between the two. In trying to mediate between the couple, she suggested to Frank that he was being ridiculous and that he should simply ignore the rumours and gossip and go back to the way his marriage had been before he had first heard them.

Frank and Emily eventually agreed to try again and, on 31 January, Frank himself penned a letter to his wife's parents to tell them that he and Emily had now sorted everything out between them. In the letter, he wrote 'Neither of us would want to part as we had love for one another' and promised to 'be as good to her as I can', telling his in-laws that 'you can both rest your hearts contented that she shan't want for anything'.

Emily's mother, Caroline Green, wrote straight back. In her letter she wrote of her concerns for her daughter, telling Frank 'God only knows what it has been to me. I do hope with all my heart that you will never say such dreadful things to her again', continuing 'no one on the face of this earth will ever make me believe that she has been unfaithful to you. She has always had too much love for you to do such a thing and I do hope that you will never be led away by others to think such a thing of her. I know her dear heart has been almost broken with the trouble she has, but I do trust that it will never occur again'.

Although Frank and Emily had agreed to give their marriage another chance, the rumours about Emily's infidelity continued unabated. Frank tried his hardest not to listen but was unable to help himself. Outwardly he maintained a façade of being a loving, caring husband, but inwardly his suspicions and jealousy were slowly but surely twisting his mind.

Matters finally came to a head on 11 February 1902. Frank and Ernest sat down at the table for tea and Frank immediately flew into a rage because Emily had not cooked fish for him. In spite of Emily's protests that today was not their day for fish and that she had cooked a perfectly good tea, Frank continued to shout and harangue her, telling her that she didn't care about him or the house but thought only of her fancy man.

Ernest was forced to intervene, receiving short shrift from Frank who told him to mind his own business. Concerned for Emily's safety and yet expected back at work, Ernest tried to extract a promise from Frank that he wouldn't hurt her after he had gone. Frank blustered and raged for a few minutes longer, before his anger finally seemed spent and he sheepishly agreed to do Emily no harm.

Reforne, Portland, 2008. (© R. Sly)

However, barely had Ernest left the house when the argument started again. Mrs Damon, who rented the other half of the house on Reforme, heard the couple yelling at each other, with Frank accusing his wife of having relations with another man and Emily strenuously denying his allegations. Eventually Emily retorted, 'If that's what you think, I'm leaving', and ran up the stairs. What Mrs Damon heard next sent chills running down her spine.

Frank calmly locked the outside door of the house and followed his wife upstairs. There were the sounds of a brief scuffle, followed by a single bloodcurdling scream.

Courageously, Mrs Damon ran to help. Finding the door to the Burdens' half of the house locked, she alerted their next-door neighbour of her fears. Mr Jonathan Lano, a local magistrate, refused point blank to interfere in a tiff between man and wife and advised Mrs Damon to refrain from doing so, ignoring her protestations that this was no ordinary quarrel.

Her attempts at getting help thus thwarted, Mrs Damon walked back towards her own home. As she did, the Burdens' front door flew open and Frank ran out, crossing the back yard and hurdling the surrounding wall. The door now open, Mrs Damon hesitantly called up the stairs, 'Missus? Missus?' Receiving no reply, she fetched a candle and bravely went up to the bedroom, where she found Emily lying half dressed on the floor in a huge pool of blood.

Mrs Damon's horrified screams finally elicited a response from Mr Lano, who rushed up the stairs, his two sons, Richard and Reginald, following him. Lano quickly took charge of the situation, sending Richard to fetch Dr Henley and Reginald to fetch the

Church Ope Cove, Portland, 1916.

local police constable. Meanwhile, he himself tried to telephone the police at Underhill, without success since, at that time, the police station was not on the telephone. Lano eventually telephoned a friend and got him to go to the island's main police station in person.

The doctor could do little but pronounce Emily Burden dead. On examination he found her to have numerous wounds on her body, including two long, deep slashes in her stomach and two cuts across her throat, which had severed her carotid artery. Since either of the wounds to her throat would have caused almost instantaneous death, it was believed that the stab wounds to Emily's stomach had been made first and she had several cuts on her hands and fingers, suggesting that she had tried in vain to grab the weapon from her attacker.

Police began a search of the island for Frank Burden, but he was not discovered until the following morning, when he was spotted crawling on his hands and knees onto the road from Church Ope Cove. After wandering around aimlessly for hours, he had tried three times during the night to drown himself, but each time had been unsuccessful. Now cold, wet and suffering from severe cramp, he had but one question for Mr Elliott, the quarryman who first found him: 'Is my wife dead?'

Assisted by a work colleague, Ambrose Stone, and a passing postman, Elliot half carried Burden to Easton Square, from where the police were called. When PC Osman arrived to collect him, Burden again asked about Emily. Having been told that she was indeed dead, Burden said that she hadn't been when he left her. He went on to explain to the policeman that, 'This is all through men going to my house while I'm away.'

On his arrest, police found the remnants of three letters that Burden had started to write to his parents but never finished. Once in custody, he sent another letter in which he told his parents:

> She drove me to kill her. She would not stop her games. Nearly drove me out of my mind. I was nearly crazy when I done it. I own up to it. I could not help myself. She was a bad one to drive me to it. I hope and trust God will forgive me. What I have done, I couldn't help myself. Dear Mother, don't worry about me for I am not worth it now. I will pray to God all the time I have in this world. I suppose everybody will cry shame at me. If they do I can't help it. All her fault. She drove me to do it. I hope and trust you won't make yourself bad over it, I wish I never seen her. Too late now. Dear Mother, if I never see you again, I hope and trust I may see you both in Heaven, for I am going to pray with all my heart for forgiveness. I hope I shall get it, but I am afraid I shan't. Give my love to all. I don't know how soon it will come. The sooner the better, for I am tired of this life.

Having appeared before magistrates at Weymouth, Frank Burden was committed to stand trial at the next Dorset Assizes for the wilful murder of his wife, Emily.

His trial opened in June 1902 and Frank pleaded 'Not Guilty' to Emily's murder. His defence counsel, Mr C.A.S Garland, had conducted some investigations into Burden's mental health and had discovered evidence of insanity in his immediate family history. On Burden's father's side of the family, Burden's uncle and his father's cousin had both been certified insane, while on his mother's side, her brother, uncle and aunt were all similarly afflicted. Burden himself had complained of suffering from severe headaches prior to killing his wife, a statement corroborated by his brother Ernest, hence it was Garland's intention to offer a defence of insanity for his client.

Burden still continued to insist that Emily had brought about her own demise by being unfaithful to him. Two doctors had examined Burden after his arrest, finding his conversation to be wandering and confused, although both differed in their opinion of his mental state. Dr Peter MacDonald, medical superintendent of the Dorset County Asylum, considered Burden to be insane. To MacDonald, the injuries to Emily Burden were so severe that only a madman could have inflicted them. Frank Burden's perceived inability to sire children and his groundless convictions that Emily was being unfaithful to him were evidence that he was delusional and, by his own testimony, had felt so ill when he killed his wife that he did not know what he was doing. Dr W.E. Good, medical officer at Dorchester Gaol, felt otherwise and was prepared to testify that Burden had shown no evidence of insanity while he was incarcerated and awaiting trial.

Accordingly, Garland had mentally prepared himself to go into court and argue against Dr Good's opinion of his client. He was therefore completely flabbergasted when the counsel for the prosecution, Mr A. Cavell Salter, seemed to want the same outcome as the defence team.

Having heard from both MacDonald and Good, who continued to disagree on the subject, the court then heard from Dr Lionel Weatherly, the medical licensee of the Bailbrook Asylum near Bath, who had been consulted by the prosecution for a third opinion. Weatherly concurred with Dr MacDonald, stating that in his opinion Burden had inherited a potentially insane mind, which had broken down when he had become stressed by his delusions of his wife's sexual affairs. Emily's 'conduct' had fast become an obsession and such delusions in a sick mind could easily produce an impulsive violent act such as suicide or murder.

At that, the judge intervened and instructed the jury to find Frank Burden guilty but insane. The jury complied and Burden was sentenced to be detained at Dorchester Prison during His Majesty's pleasure.

No evidence was ever found to support Burden's assertions that he was infertile. Ironically, just weeks before killing his wife, Frank Burden had been offered a job as a keeper to a titled gentleman. Emily had strongly urged him to accept, but he had refused because he preferred to stay in the Portland area, close to his family. Had Burden accepted the job and moved away then it was possible that Emily's life would have been spared.

[Note: In various contemporary accounts of the murder of Emily Burden, some variations of names appear. The Burdens' lodger, Jack Roberts, is alternatively referred to as John Roberts. Their neighbour is alternately called John and Jonathan Lano. The two men alleged to have had an affair with Emily Burden, Abe Winter and his friend John (Jack) Pearce, were the Burden's rent collector and a monumental mason. In some accounts Winter is referred to as the rent collector and Pearce as the stonemason – in other accounts their positions have been reversed.]

10

'I DON'T WANT ANYTHING ELSE TO DO WITH YOU, MR SIMMONS'

Weymouth, 1902

There was, Dr Pritzler Wetherall decided, something seriously wrong with his patient. The man had come to his surgery that morning complaining of vomiting and of being unable to sleep. However, as the doctor tried to question him, Edward Simmons refused to sit down, nervously pacing and babbling incessantly about anything and everything, making it almost impossible for the doctor to get a word in edgeways.

After several unsuccessful attempts at breaking into the man's monologue, the doctor had had enough. Casting a glance at Simmons's wife, who sat quietly in a corner of the surgery anxiously watching her husband's bizarre behaviour, Wetherall suddenly bellowed 'Sit Down!' The order was enough to stop Simmons in his tracks for just long enough for the doctor to briefly examine him, diagnose alcoholic gastritis and prescribe some medicine.

When he next visited the surgery, Simmons was given short shrift by the doctor who had checked up on some of his ramblings from his first visit and found them to be a pack of lies. Simmons was not the ex-medical student he had claimed to be, nor did he have a brother in the Army Medical Corps. Excusing his brevity by saying that he had an urgent appointment, Wetherall dispensed some more medicine and ushered Simmons and his wife politely, but firmly, from his surgery.

The truth was that Simmons had suffered a severe illness as a child and his parents had been warned that he would most probably be left with some permanent mental disability as a result. Although he was undoubtedly a sickly child, suffering from frequent fainting spells, he did well at school and on leaving was employed by a firm of wholesale druggists. He initially did very well at his new job but, within a short time, he became convinced that the foreman did not like him and was deliberately picking on him.

He began to take unscheduled time off work and eventually just seemed to disappear into thin air. His parents were frantic with worry, wondering if this was the onset of the mental disability that they had been warned about many years earlier. In a desperate effort to find their son, they placed advertisements in national newspapers, asking for anyone who had seen Edward to contact them.

They were surprised by the response that the advertisement elicited. Writing in the third person, Edward himself replied. It was obvious that he had absolutely no memory of events that had occurred since he left his job for the very last time.

When he was safely home again, a family conference was called to decide what to do about Edward and it was at this point that his brother John, usually known as Jack, had a brainwave, announcing that he would give Edward a job. Edward was smart and cultured, said Jack, with a pleasant personality and the 'gift of the gab' – he would make an excellent travelling salesman.

It seemed as though Edward had finally found his niche. Jack was delighted with his brother's performance, particularly since he firmly believed that the downfall of travelling salesmen was alcohol and Edward was a staunch teetotaller.

Or at least he was until he met up with a group of commercial travellers in a hotel in Cardiff. On learning that Edward planned to spend the evening balancing his books in his room, the salesmen were appalled and managed to persuade him to take the night off and come for a drink. Edward agreed, having first stipulated that he would take nothing alcoholic. He failed to notice that the group were spiking his drinks and was soon drunk to the point of passing out.

He woke up the next morning with a terrible hangover and was horrified to realise that, while he had been dead to the world, his brother's samples had been stolen, as had all the money he had collected on his trip and the contents of his own wallet.

Edward was far too ashamed to go home. Instead, he wrote to Jack begging his forgiveness and apologising over and over again for letting him down. He ended the letter by saying that he planned to go to Ireland and join the Army.

He served for eight years with the West Kent Regiment, achieving the rank of sergeant and travelling all over the world. Apart from a brief spell in hospital in India, his health improved dramatically and he was eventually discharged with an exemplary service record.

Once he had left the Army, Edward became the manager of a late-night club in Edinburgh, before moving to Manchester to manage a similar club for the same owners. In 1895 he married his wife, Frances, and the couple later adopted a child.

By this time Simmons was beginning to exhibit some rather strange behaviour. He constantly complained of headaches and was certain that the top of his head was

The Harbour, Weymouth, 1954.

about to come off. The loving and indulgent Frances would spend many hours humouring her husband by holding the top of his head in order to prevent such an occurrence.

When Frances herself became ill and was hospitalised for a lengthy period, Edward seemed lost without her. He began to show up for work at the club earlier and earlier, forcing his staff to do the same. Indeed, he was often observed sitting on the steps of the club in his pyjamas in the early hours of the morning. Despite his obvious problems, his employers were still more than happy with the way that he ran the club, but, once again, Simmons began to have delusions that they were deliberately interfering with his job because they didn't like him. His paranoia grew to the point where he felt obliged to hand in his notice. The club management turned down his first two letters of resignation, but finally accepted his third, leaving him not only jobless but homeless as well.

When Frances was finally discharged from hospital, the couple moved to Aldershot to stay with friends until, after five weeks, Simmons secured the post of steward/secretary for the Royal Dorset Yacht Club at Weymouth.

Simmons obviously still possessed his 'gift for the gab', since he quickly made friends with several people in his new hometown, including the Graham family, partners in a large firm of wine merchants. The Yacht Club was close to Graham & Sons wine bar and Edward got into the habit of popping in regularly for a drink, usually a ginger ale, but occasionally he would take a glass of whisky. Soon he became completely enamoured by one of the barmaids who worked there, twenty-four-year-old Hettie Stephens from Truro, Cornwall.

A little flirting from customers is an occupational hazard for barmaids, particularly when they are as attractive as Hettie. However, Hettie was certainly not interested in any

57

The Harbour, Weymouth, 1931.

male attention, since she already had a steady boyfriend, who was currently working the Klondyke Gold Rush to make enough money for them to marry.

Eventually Simmons purchased a gold bracelet for Hettie, the latest in a series of small gifts, paying £2 7s 6d for it from a local jeweller. He persuaded the jeweller to write him a receipt for £2 10s 0d and, having given Hettie the bracelet in the bar one evening, then proceeded to make a big show about how much it had cost him.

Hettie had never shown any interest in Simmons beyond the obligatory politeness from a barmaid to a paying customer. Not wishing to offend him by refusing the bracelet, she accepted it and thanked him, but coolly continued to keep her distance.

His lack of success with Hettie was not all that was troubling Simmons at that time, as he had become convinced that mail was being stolen from the yacht club. Although the intended recipient of the letters had made no complaint, Simmons involved the police, who, after spending countless hours investigating the alleged theft, came to the conclusion that the crime existed only in the mind of Edward Simmons. Many of the friends he had initially made on his arrival in Weymouth were now beginning to draw away from Simmons, believing him to be opinionated, argumentative, a braggart and a habitual liar.

The slightest untoward incident threw Simmons into an emotional turmoil. He was driven almost to the point of a nervous breakdown when a man spoke to him at a concert without first being introduced and, on another occasion, the sight of a man wearing a woman's bracelet was enough to send him into near meltdown. Concerned for her husband's mental health, Frances took the unusual step of consulting Dr Wetherall alone, tearfully begging the doctor to do something. Wetherall calmed her, promising that he would sort something out.

Weymouth in the 1930s.

Edward's next step was to call on Percy Graham and ask him for a private word on a rather delicate matter. He told Percy that he had watched Hettie Stephens pocketing money from the till in the wine bar and that he had also seen her drunk in charge of the bar several times. Graham realised that these allegations could not possibly be true and demanded that Simmons leave his office immediately, warning him not to repeat the preposterous allegations against Hettie to anyone else.

Simmons went straight from Graham's office to the local ironmongers, where he asked to see some really sharp knives, explaining that he needed one for sticking pigs. He eventually purchased one with a 5in blade, then, leaving the ironmongers, hailed a taxi and asked to be driven to the railway station. Arthur Collins drove him to the station, and then returned to the taxi rank on the Esplanade where, by chance, he immediately picked up another fare for the station. As he drove, he spotted Simmons walking back into town and wondered why he had asked for a cab, only to immediately turn round on reaching his destination and return. Later, Collins was to find the brand new knife that Simmons had just purchased under the seat cushions in his taxi.

Simmons went straight to the shops on his return to Weymouth town centre and purchased a revolver for 'shooting rats'. Having rejected the first gun he was shown because it was too big, he bought a smaller gun, only to return it to the shop minutes later because it was too small, finally settling on the gun he had first turned down. He then asked for ammunition, but was told that he needed to go to Mr Hayman's shop, a little further along the street. At that, Simmon's walked out and went straight to Mr Lanning's shop, where he again demanded ammunition. Never having stocked ammunition, Lanning also directed him to Hayman's, but Simmons lingered in Lanning's shop and eventually purchased another knife almost identical to the one he had just left in the taxi. He never did manage to reach Hayman's.

Weymouth locals watched as Simmons's behaviour became ever more bizarre. On one occasion he was observed walking out of the yacht club and slamming the door behind him, only to do an immediate about turn and go back inside again. He repeated this sequence of actions over and over again, until the watchers tired of looking at him and went off to do something else, leaving him still going in and out, in and out, in and out . . .

Simmon's preoccupation with Hettie Stephens's alleged wrongdoings became an obsession, related in detail to anyone who was prepared to listen to him. Most people ignored him, including his wife, but others went to the Grahams with what they had been told, eventually forcing Percy Graham to approach Frances Simmons on the street and ask her to get her husband to stop blackening the girl's character.

Embarrassed, Frances agreed to have word with her husband, but she didn't get the chance. It came to the notice of Archie Graham that Simmons was spreading rumours about Hettie and he confronted Simmons in the wine bar and told him in no uncertain terms that it must stop. Simmons admitted that he had been wrong and promised that he wouldn't say another word against Hettie.

By now, in a very fragile mental state and almost totally unable to sleep, the slightest irritation was sufficient to send Simmons over the top. When a member brought a dog into the yacht club, against the rules, he screamed and ranted like a lunatic. He was more convinced than ever that the top of his head was coming off and poor Frances had to spend hours holding it in place for him.

Still unable to go to Hayman's shop to buy ammunition himself, he eventually sent the hall porter from the yacht club to buy some for him, then attempted to load the gun by pushing the bullets into the trigger aperture, throwing a tantrum when they wouldn't fit and sending the porter back to the shop to exchange the 'wrongly sized' bullets. The porter wisely got some instructions on how to load the gun and passed them on to Simmons. Between them, they managed to load the weapon and Simmons fired a test shot in the table tennis room of the club.

On 27 March 1902, Simmons asked the night porter at the yacht club to deliver a note to Hettie Stephens for him, stressing that he should wait for a reply and not to return without one. The porter duly obliged. The note asked Hettie to meet Simmons so that they could discuss the things he had been saying about her and, presumably anxious to clear her name, Hettie sent back a note agreeing to meet him in the bar that evening.

She was due for a tea break at 6 p.m. but when that time came, her replacement had not yet arrived, so she continued to look after the bar. Simmons walked in and immediately began, what looked to other customers, an argument with Hettie. They could not discern exactly what was being said but, on one occasion, Hettie raised her voice in anger and the words 'Not after what you said about me' were heard.

When her relief, Edith Hill, arrived at 6.15 p.m., the argument seemed to have run its course. Edith heard Hettie tell Simmons, 'I don't want anything else to do with you, Mr Simmons', at which point Hettie went to the small cloakroom at the end of the bar, got her coat and put it on ready to leave.

As Hettie walked across the bar towards the door, three shots rang out. Edith screamed as Hettie fell instantly to the floor, having taken all three bullets in the face. Then, as Edith and the bar customers looked on in horror, Simmons put the barrel of the revolver into his mouth and pulled the trigger once more. The bullet came straight out through Simmons's cheek, before embedding itself in the ceiling of the bar.

The police and a doctor were sent for and the customers in the bar courageously tackled Simmons who meekly passed his gun to one of them, saying, 'Don't fret. I've done what I intended to do and I'll wait quietly until the police arrive.'

Simmons was taken to Weymouth police station, where a doctor was called to attend to his injuries. It was Dr Wetherall and Simmons greeted him like an old friend. He was apparently unable to comprehend that he had done anything wrong, joking when the doctor was forced to shave off part of his moustache to stitch his wounds and asking if the doctor would mind going back to the wine bar for him, as he seemed to have left his false teeth there. (The teeth were later found scattered all around the bar, having been shattered by the bullet.)

Although Simmons stood trial for the murder of Hettie Stephens, it was obvious to all concerned that he was certifiably insane. The trial opened at Dorchester in June 1902 before Mr Justice Bucknill and lasted for three days. Having heard all the evidence put before them, the jury quickly returned a verdict of 'Guilty', but with the rider that Simmons was not responsible for his actions at the time of the shooting by reason of insanity. He was ordered to be detained at an asylum during his Majesty's pleasure.

11

'GOD BLESS YOU AND KEEP YOU, DEARIE'

Southbourne, 1908

On 20 February 1908, a group of boys from Mount Pleasant School were out walking with their teacher on the cliffs at Southbourne when they spotted a woman lying apparently asleep in the grass. Thinking it was rather too cold a day for sunbathing, the boys hurried to tell their teacher, Robert Spurgeon, what they had seen. Spurgeon dismissed their chatter and insisted that the walk continue, but when the woman was still there on their return, he decided that he should take a closer look.

At first glance, it was evident that not only was the woman dead, but that she had not died of natural causes. Her neck was marked and the backs of both of her hands were scratched, as if she had tried to fight off an attacker. Two handkerchiefs were balled up and stuffed into her mouth.

Spurgeon called over another rambler, who agreed to stand guard over the body while Spurgeon went for help and removed his young charges from the scene of the crime. Spurgeon then went to the nearby coastguard station to report what he and the boys had found.

The police arrived at the scene, already having a theory about the possible identity of the body. The previous day, thirty-six-year-old Emma Sherriff had been reported missing from her lodgings in Palmerston Road, Boscombe, having not been seen for two days. Their theory was quickly confirmed.

Emma Sheriff was a rather frail woman who did not always enjoy the best of health. After years of working in service, she had received an inheritance of £600 and now lived off the income from her nest egg, supplemented with money that she earned with

Mount Pleasant School, Southbourne-on-Sea, 1917.

her skills as a dressmaker. She was a religious woman, regularly attending services at St John's Mission Hall in Boscombe, and it was there that she formed a close circle of female friends.

Probably the best of those friends was widow Annie McGuire, who was a nurse. Annie lived in Tower Road and Emma often stayed overnight at her friend's house, even occasionally sleeping in Annie's bed when she was working the night shift. Annie shared her home with her son, John Francis McGuire, who was always known as Frank. Emma had known Frank, who was fifteen years her junior, since he was a boy and he was in fact her only male friend.

Frank had served in the Army since 1903, first in the Royal Artillery, then in the Horseguards and finally in the Lifeguards. Whenever he was on leave he would travel back to Bournemouth to visit his mother and, while he was there, it seemed his friendship with Emily might have developed into an intimate relationship. Emma often stayed overnight at the McGuire's home, even when Annie was working. She would always ask the McGuire's landlady, Amelia Galpin, not to tell Annie that she and Frank had been together in the living room all night with the lights out and Mrs Galpin complied, feeling that whatever the couple did behind closed doors was none of her business.

In 1906, to the consternation of both his mother and Emily, Frank apparently disappeared. He stopped visiting and his regular letters home ceased abruptly. Despite their combined efforts, Annie and Emma were unable to find any trace of him until, in January 1908, Emma finally received a letter from Frank, in which he apologised for not being in touch and asked if he could visit her in Bournemouth.

Tower Road, Boscombe, 2008. (© N. Sly)

In spite of Frank's request in the letter that Emma didn't mention anything to his mother, Annie was the first person that Emma told. Having given up nursing and gone into service, Annie had left the house in Tower Road for a live-in position in Boscombe. Hence, Emma arranged with her own landlady in Palmerston Road, Mary Lane, for a room to be set aside for Frank's use when he visited. Annie warned her that Frank was no longer a boy and that there may be talk, but Emma was unconcerned by the prospect, saying that she was a grown woman and could do as she liked.

Having made arrangements for his visit, Emma wrote back to Frank, using her own special nickname for him;

> My dearest Sonny, You can't know or think how welcome your letter was this morning after so long, as we didn't know what had happened to you. Dearest Sonny, you must forgive me. I had to tell dear mother the good news I have from you. It has been a dreadful time of anxiety for us both and I couldn't help telling her to relieve her mind. You must forgive me betraying your confidence.

The letter was signed 'God bless you and keep you, dearie. Fondest love, from your ever loving, sister Emmie' [*sic*].

Frank arrived in Boscombe on 7 February 1908 and moved into Emma's lodgings. He was originally intending to stay for a week, but extended his stay until 17 February. He and Emma went out together several times and, as he was leaving to catch his train back to Waterloo, Mary Lane jokingly asked him if he planned to take Emma with him. 'No, not yet', replied McGuire.

Palmerston Road, Boscombe, 2008. (© N. Sly)

When Emma returned to her lodgings after seeing Frank off at the station, she was shocked to find some of her personal belongings were missing. Her gold locket and chain, a bracelet and her savings of around £5 were nowhere to be found. Although Frank had gone to London on the afternoon train, he was planning on returning to Christchurch that evening and Emma had arranged to meet him at a crossroads in Soutbourne at 7.30 p.m. Emma confided to a friend, Lily Hatch, that she intended to confront him about the missing items, urging, 'Don't say anything to anyone until I've seen him.'

Lily saw Emma again the following morning and asked how the evening had gone. Emma told her that Frank had said that he had taken the items as a joke and was planning to return them that evening, but had left them in his bag at Christchurch. He had promised to bring them back the following day and arranged to meet Emma for dinner at midday.

While Emma was talking to Lily, a letter was delivered to her lodgings and Mary Lane gave it to her when she returned at just after eleven o'clock. Mrs Lane saw Emma again at one o'clock, at which time she thought that Emma looked rather upset. Then, later that evening, she heard Emma lock the door of her room and go out.

Emma didn't return that night, but Mrs Lane assumed that she was staying with a friend. The next morning, Wednesday 19 February, a telegram arrived for Emma and Mrs Lane took it up to her room. She found the door locked and the window blinds drawn down.

Worried, she sent her niece to see Annie McGuire, but Emma had not stayed the night with her. On hearing that Emma had not been seen since the previous day, Mrs McGuire decided to open the telegram. It was from her son, Frank, and read simply: 'Meet me at three o'clock at Boscombe'.

Mrs McGuire went straight round to Emma's lodgings in Palmerston Road. Shortly after she arrived, Frank also turned up, followed by Lily Hatch and another friend of Emma's, Mrs Carroll. Mrs Lane led everyone upstairs to Emma's rooms and when a spare key could not be located, she instructed Frank to break down the door. When they gained entrance to the room, Emma's friends found that her bed hadn't been slept in.

Lily Hatch managed to steal a quick word with Annie McGuire. 'You have been deceived', she whispered. 'There has more been going on between Frank and her than you know of. You thought Frank went back to London on Monday, but he didn't.' Annie McGuire was disbelieving. She had received a letter from Frank that very morning, clearly posted in London the night before. In it Frank had written that he and Emma had made plans to go to the theatre on Wednesday evening that week and asked if she would like to come too.

Annie McGuire sent Frank to check the hospital and to report Emma's disappearance to the police and, when he had left, continued her conversation with Lily Hatch. She learned about the missing jewellery and money and that Frank had spent Monday night staying at the Salisbury Hotel, Boscombe, rather than in London, as she had thought.

Meanwhile, Frank McGuire was at Boscombe police station enquiring whether there had been an accident involving a woman. He explained to the officers that he had made arrangements to meet a lady that afternoon but that she hadn't kept their appointment, nor had she been seen at her lodgings since the previous day. He told police that he was a businessman and that he would be returning to London at 11.30 a.m. the following day, promising to call back and leave his name and address if Emma hadn't been traced by then. The police officers thought that he seemed nervous, pale and shaken, but they reasoned that reporting a friend as a missing person was likely to upset anyone.

Frank stayed the night at the Salisbury Hotel, having first had to answer some questions from his mother. He admitted to her that he had stayed in Boscombe on the Monday night and hung his head when his mother confronted him about Emma's missing belongings. Mrs McGuire thought that Emma may have travelled to London to see Frank in order to try and retrieve her money and jewellery, so she asked Frank to send a reply paid telegram to his London lodgings to ask if a woman had called there for him. Frank sent the telegram on his way to the station and later a reply arrived at his mother's house saying that nobody had called.

Soon afterwards, Annie McGuire heard that a woman's body had been found on Southbourne Cliffs. When the identity of the body was confirmed as Emma, Mrs McGuire sent a telegram to Emma's mother, Jesse Lavers of Plymouth.

Mrs Lavers took the next train, arriving at Palmerston Road to be told by Mrs Lane that her daughter had been 'done to death'. Annie McGuire, however, firmly believed that Emma had committed suicide. She was unable to acknowledge the truth behind Emma's tragic demise since, had Emma been murdered, then the most logical suspect would have been her beloved son, Frank. When questioned by police, she continued to insist that Frank had been in London on 18 February, showing them the postmarked letter from him as proof.

Officers from the Metropolitan Police Force were at Frank McGuire's London address within a day of the discovery of Emma's body, requested by their colleagues in Bournemouth to detain him. Frank was charged with Emma's murder and brought back to Bournemouth for questioning.

The inquest into Emma's death opened on 22 February. A post-mortem examination, conducted by police surgeon Dr Harold Simmons, revealed that she had numerous injuries including a broken rib and flattening of the left-hand side of her chest, severe bruising to the abdomen and internal bleeding from her stomach, spleen and bowels. Dr Simmons believed that death was due to this internal bleeding coupled with shock and estimated that Emma Sherriff would have lived for between ten and twenty minutes after the injuries had been inflicted. He was unsure exactly what had caused the injuries but suggested that she had either been kicked, punched, kneed or struck repeatedly with a blunt instrument.

As the inquest progressed, more became known about Frank's mysterious life in London. He had deserted from the Army eighteen months previously and formed an allegiance with a retired officer, Major Powell Moore. Such was their relationship that McGuire often called himself Powell and the Major referred to him as 'my son', even showing people pictures of his dead wife, telling them that this was 'Frank's mother'.

McGuire had been working as a picture dealer in Pimlico, buying pictures from artists at a set price and selling them on to galleries, keeping any profit. His main client was an artist called Henry Hayman from Rochester. Hayman knew him as Frank Powell and 'Powell' was actually engaged to be married to his daughter. That McGuire was having financial difficulties was evidenced by the pawn tickets relating to pictures and paintings that were found when police searched his London rooms.

As well as insights into Frank's life, the inquest brought forth new information about Emma. She was known to be an extremely tidy woman, yet after her death her friend Susan Royce found the missing jewellery and money wrapped in a handkerchief in a box under her bed, rather than in her jewellery box where they were usually kept. Likewise, her purse and handbag were found in her room, also not in their proper place. Had someone hurriedly replaced them after her murder?

Frederick Blachford, a bootmaker's boy from Boscombe, gave evidence at the inquest. He related how, on the morning of 18 February, McGuire had paid him 6d to deliver a letter to Miss Sherriff at Palmerston Road.

When the inquest ended with a verdict of wilful murder, the jury made a point of stating that grave suspicions were attached to Frank McGuire. Having appeared before Bournemouth magistrates in a committal hearing that lasted four days, McGuire was sent for trial at the next Hampshire Assizes.

The trial opened at Winchester Castle on 28 May 1908 before Mr Justice A.C. Lawrence, with Mr F.R.Y. Radcliffe QC prosecuting and Mr J.A. Hawke defending. The 6ft tall McGuire looked every inch the ex-soldier as he stood in the dock while the charge against him was read, pleading 'Not Guilty' in a clear, confident voice.

Radcliffe opened with the details of Emma's death, stating that she died between 7 p.m. and 8.30 p.m. on 18 February and that her death was either due to her being kicked or a person deliberately falling upon her, landing heavily on her left-hand side on his or her knees.

The counsel for the prosecution then went on to stress the seriousness of Frank McGuire's financial problems. As well as the pawn tickets found in his room, letters between McGuire and his fiancée, Alice Hayman, were produced in court in which money problems were discussed. It appeared that McGuire had also stolen some of Alice's jewellery, which was later recovered from a London pawnbroker. Radcliffe was unable to question Lily Hatch about Emma Sheriff's missing jewellery, since the conversation between them would have been hearsay and consequently inadmissible as evidence. However, he did elicit the information that jewellery had been found concealed in Emma's room in places where she would never normally have kept it.

He drew the conclusion that someone had been in possession of certain articles belonging to Emma and had replaced them in her room after her death. Her handbag, purse and most of her jewellery were not found on her body but instead were found in the most unlikely places in her room after her death. Radcliffe asked who could reasonably have replaced the items, drawing the conclusion that McGuire was the most likely suspect.

The prosecution then called a key witness, an Armerian lady, Mrs Phoebe Nutter-Scott. Mrs Nutter-Scott had been on a tramcar at around eight o'clock on the evening of the murder and had seen a man boarding the car at Broad Street in Southbourne. The man was breathing heavily and appeared pale, his hat pulled over his eyes as if he did not want to be recognised. He stood out because, like McGuire, he was very tall, and Mrs Nutter-Scott later picked McGuire in an identity parade.

Mr Hawke, for the defence, tried to insinuate that Mrs Nutter-Scott suffered from mental illness but she stood up to his cross-examination very well until its conclusion, when she slowly subsided to the floor in a faint. She was carried from the courtroom.

The main contention of the defence was that McGuire was in London at the time of the murder and so could not have killed Emma. Indeed, his landlady had seen him there and was thus able to substantiate his alibi, and there was also the matter of the London postmark on the letter he sent to his mother. Radcliffe suggested that, after paying the Boscombe boot boy to deliver his letter, McGuire had caught a train from Boscombe to Waterloo, arriving at Clapham at 1.22 p.m. and reaching Victoria shortly after 1.30 p.m. A London boot boy, Sidney Wingrove, gave evidence that he had cleaned McGuire's shoes at 2 p.m. that afternoon and that afterwards McGuire had given him two letters to post, with instructions not to post them until after 8 p.m.

Radcliffe then called the daughter of McGuire's London landlady, who had managed to lock herself out of the house and testified that McGuire had let her in when he arrived home at midnight on the night of the murder.

However, Radcliffe suggested that McGuire had actually left London at 4.10 p.m., arriving in Bournemouth in time to meet Emma Sherriff at 6.30 p.m. Having murdered her, he then caught the 8.50 p.m. train back to London which gave him plenty of time to get back to his lodgings by midnight.

Radcliffe produced two letters which had been found in McGuire's pockets when he was arrested; one was addressed to Emma, the other to his mother, and both were written on paper similar to that found in Emma's room. The envelopes were addressed but not posted, and in them Frank announced his safe return to London. What, asked Radcliffe, was the purpose of these letters? He suggested that Frank had intended to commit the murder on Monday 17 February and that these letters were written for the sole purpose of establishing an alibi for the relevant period but not posted when the murder had not taken place as planned.

Frank McGuire had a simple explanation. Called to the witness stand, he maintained that he had written them well before leaving Bournemouth in order to save time and had just forgotten to post them. He told the court that he had last met Emma on the evening of Monday 17 February and had returned to London the following morning, the day on which she met her death. He had met Wingrove, the boot boy, at 3 p.m. and given him sixpence for posting his letters the previous day, not on the day of the murder. He had wanted to conceal from his mother the fact that he was in Bournemouth on the Monday night; hence he had asked the boy to post the letters after 8 p.m. that evening.

He denied arriving at his lodgings at midnight on Tuesday 18 February, saying that his landlady's daughter had been mistaken. Finally, he reiterated that he had not met Emma Sherriff at the crossroads on Tuesday and had definitely not seen her at all that day.

'So you did not murder her?' Mr Hawke asked him.

'I did not', replied McGuire firmly.

The jury retired at 7.50 p.m. on the third day of the trial but, after a little more than an hour, sent a message to say that they were hopelessly deadlocked. They were asked to continue deliberating for a further two hours to see if the stalemate could be resolved.

At eleven o'clock they had still failed to reach a unanimous verdict and told the judge that they believed that there was not the slightest chance that they would be able to reach agreement. This left the judge with no choice but to dismiss them and to remand Frank McGuire in custody until the next Assizes, when he would face a retrial. However, the retrial never happened.

On 25 June, the Attorney General, Sir William Robson, entered a *Nolle Prosequi* after having received 'new evidence' on the case. For reasons that have never been revealed, the charges against Frank McGuire were dropped and he was released from prison on 27 June 1908, a free man.

In an interview given to the *Bournemouth Echo* after his release, he thanked his legal representatives and praised his jailers for always treating him as the innocent man he was. He thanked the anonymous donor of a gift of £10, sent to him shortly after the trial, and announced his intention of accepting the offer of another anonymous benefactor, who had promised to set him up in a picture business in any English town he chose. He had chosen Tunbridge Wells, he told the reporter. He failed to mention that, as an innocent man, he would also now benefit from a £100 legacy left to him by Emma Sherriff in her will.

Surviving documents on the case contain no clues as to the nature of the 'new evidence' that secured McGuire's freedom. However, it is believed that the original trial jury had voted 10–2 in favour of McGuire's acquittal, so it is possible that the Attorney General simply wished to avoid the expense of another trial that could easily have ended in the acquittal of the accused. No other person has ever been prosecuted in connection with the murder of Emma Sherriff and, officially, the case remains unsolved to this day.

12

'SHE DOESN'T WANT ANY MONEY WHERE SHE IS TO'

Gussage St Michael, 1913

William Walter Burton was a dapper young man who was seen as a cut above the normal Dorset farm worker. Married to an older woman, who ran the post office at Gussage St Michael and also taught at the village school, he was the very picture of respectability – a regular churchgoer who sang in the choir and was also a bell ringer.

Burton worked as a rabbit trapper and, at Manor Farm, Gussage St Michael, he met twenty-three-year-old cook, Winifred Mary Mitchell, who was actually a distant relation of his by marriage. Winnie, as she was known, was an attractive brunette with a sweet face and a petite but curvy figure. She was a lively, fun-loving young woman who soon found herself strongly attracted to the rugged and virile Burton with his athletic body, sandy hair and neat moustache.

The couple met regularly at their work and quickly became friends, then lovers, although Winnie apparently baulked at taking the final steps to physical intimacy. Letters were exchanged between them and, reading between the lines, it seems certain that Burton used a degree of emotional blackmail to finally coerce her into submission. In one letter he wrote that he knew that she would be cross and upset because she had said that she would never forgive such a nasty thing as had happened the previous day. The nature of the 'nasty thing' seems apparent, as the letter continued to say that her love for him was not very strong. He had proved that he loved her and they had been together long enough to know each other. In other words, 'if you loved me, you would sleep with me', and Winnie obviously eventually capitulated to Burton's demands, because, in 1913, she told him that she was pregnant.

To Winnie, Burton said exactly the words she wanted to hear. They would be married, he promised. Perhaps they would elope to London, or even Canada. However, behind Winnie's back, Burton's true feelings were revealed to his friend, Arthur Bush. To Arthur, Burton confided that he wished he could find some young man to court Winnie and take the blame for her pregnancy. Winnie's mother, Rose Mitchell, was told only part of the story. Winnie was going away and she would contact her mother as soon as she arrived at her hitherto unknown destination.

Between them, the two lovers hatched a plan. Winnie was to pack her clothes – and some of Burton's – in her travelling bag. A car was to collect her from a crossroads near the farm and drive her to Wimborne station, where she would catch the mail train to London. Burton would make his own way to London to avoid arousing suspicion and the couple would then meet up with friends who lived in the capital.

Burton confided this plan to another friend, carter Fred Butt. Butt was horrified and urged Burton to reconsider, telling him that if he went the police would surely be after him. Burton told him that he planned to shave off his moustache as a disguise and that, if he went, he did not plan on returning to Gussage St Michael ever again. 'I'm not so sure about that', replied Butt, sagely.

However, Butt's warning seemed to have struck a chord with Burton and, the next time he saw Winnie, he told her that he had changed his mind and would not be going away with her. Winnie was understandably furious with him for going back on his promise. She threatened to reveal her pregnancy to Burton's wife, not to mention details of Burton's previous affairs with other women.

Lily Burton had not the slightest inkling about her husband's affair with the young cook, nor was she aware that there had been several other dalliances in the past. For a man like Burton, seen as a pillar of his local community, the inevitable consequences of such revelations were unthinkable.

On 31 March 1913, Winnie finished her dinner at Manor Farm at 2 p.m., then dressed herself in her best clothes, putting on what few trinkets of jewellery she possessed. At 2.55 p.m., she mounted her bicycle and rode off towards the village. Coincidentally, the first person she met on her journey was Lily Burton and the two women chatted for a few moments before Winnie rode on. She was seen by a villager a few minutes later talking to William Burton, who was sitting on some railings. It was the last time she would be seen alive by anyone other than her killer.

At first, her disappearance didn't cause too much alarm in the village since it was known that she had already told her mother that she would be leaving. Still, tongues wagged and rumours spread about her possible whereabouts, with William Burton happy to add to the gossip, telling people that he had heard that she had gone to London or to Canada and that he knew she was all right because she had contacted her family.

However, as well as reassuring villagers about Winnie's safety, William Burton also made some rather odd remarks. He remarked to Winifred Bailey, another servant at Manor Farm, that if the police found Winnie in the plantation, he would take his oath that he had done nothing to her. Brewer's drayman Frank Christopher was told by Burton that Winnie had left all her money behind, but that it didn't matter because 'She doesn't want any money where she is to' [*sic*]. Burton also visited Winnie's mother to see if she had heard any news of her daughter and, a couple of weeks later, he was responsible for starting a rumour that 'Cookie' had been found in London.

On 30 April, police were summoned to the cottage of George Gillingham by the rector of Gussage St Michael, the Revd Wright. Some weeks before, George, who worked as a dairyman at Manor Farm, had been walking with his wife in Sovell Plantation, a nearby wood, when they had found a broken set of false teeth. They had picked the teeth up and brought them home, not realising their possible significance. However, the rector was aware that Winnie wore dentures and was quick to notify the police when he spotted the teeth on the Gillingham's mantelpiece.

Police began to investigate and soon found two young boys who believed that they had seen an open grave in Sovell plantation the day before Winnie went missing. Searching for primroses, they had stumbled across a large hole that was 5 or 6ft long and about 2ft deep. A large pile of earth and an abandoned spade lay beside the hole.

On 2 May, one of the boys, Henry Palmer, led police to the site of the hole, which had since been filled in and covered with some branches. Sergeant James Stockley poked the ground with a stick and, when it was withdrawn from the soil, he noticed that it bore traces of human hair.

Police dug down and, eighteen inches below the surface of the ground, located the body of a young woman buried face down. A veil covered her face but it was still possible to recognise the body as that of Winifred Mitchell. Her long coat was undone and some of her underwear was missing. Most of her head had been blown away, apparently by a shotgun, and another piece from her false teeth was located near to her grave.

Since Burton was the last person known to have seen Winnie alive, police went straight to Manor Farm and arrested him on suspicion of murder. They had already heard that, on 31 March, Burton had borrowed a gun on the pretext of shooting a black and white cat belonging to Fred Boyt. The gun had been returned a couple of hours later and it's owner, Leonard Mitcham, was warned not to tell anyone that Burton had had the gun all afternoon, but to say instead that they had walked to the top of a nearby hill together and shot at some pigeons. Although Burton had told Mitcham that he had successfully shot the cat, it was in fact very much alive.

Its owner could testify to that. And Boyt was also able to tell the police that, on the evening of Winnie's disappearance, Burton had tapped on the window of his cottage and asked Boyt to come with him to Sovell Plantation where he wanted to check some traps. The two had walked together to a bridle path leading to the woods, then Burton had left Boyt for a few minutes. When he returned, he was pushing a woman's bicycle, which he told Boyt belonged to Winnie.

Winnie had gone to Canada, he continued and he had promised to return her bicycle to her mother's home. Boyt was warned that if he ever said anything to anyone about the bicycle then it would be a 'bad job' for him, a warning that was repeated several times over the next few weeks.

View from Cranborne church tower, 1930s.

When the police arrived to arrest him, Burton's first question to Sergeant Stockley was 'Have you found her?' When Stockley said yes, Burton paled, saying that he knew he would be blamed as it had been said that he was the last person to be seen with her. He then burst into tears.

Taken to Cranborne police station, Burton expressed concern for his wife and said that it was a shame that he had ever set eyes on Winnie Mitchell. He denied killing her, saying that when he had met her at three o'clock she had told him that she was going to Lower Gussage, and that she had been alive and well when he left her. He intimated that he was merely one of a number of men who should be suspected of murdering Winnie, the obvious implication being that the young cook had been rather free with her favours. If the police would only release him, he told PC Anderson, he could find plenty of men who could support his story. Furthermore, he assured Superintendent Ricketts that he could account for every single minute of his time on the afternoon when Winnie went missing.

Burton appeared before magistrates at Wimborne on 21 May, charged with the wilful murder of Winifred Mary Mitchell. He pleaded 'Not Guilty' but was committed for trial at the next Dorset Assizes, which opened in Dorchester on 1 June 1913 before Mr Justice Ridley.

The court heard from Fred Boyt and Leonard Mitcham, who repeated their statements to the police and also from Rose Mitchell, who told of finding her daughter's bicycle leaning against a tree in her garden after Winnie's disappearance. In the soft earth next to the bike was a footprint made by a man's hobnail boot, similar to those usually worn by Burton.

On the second and last day of the trial, Burton himself was put into the witness box. Asked to account for his movements on the day of the murder, he said that he was setting traps until 2 p.m. when he met Mitcham and suggested that they went shooting. The two had walked together up a hill and Burton had fired two cartridges, one at a thrush. Mitcham then left him with the gun, which he put into a nearby pit. Seeing his wife talking to Winnie Mitchell, he had joined them and chatted for a while, after which Winnie had ridden off on her bicycle towards Gussage All Saints. Burton had then returned to his work until it was time to go home, when he had retrieved the gun and returned it to Mitcham. In the evening, he, Mitcham and Boyt had walked up the hill together and he had found the bicycle behind a hayrick. According to Burton, Boyt had been the one to put the bicycle in Mrs Mitchell's garden.

Burton denied ever having had sexual relations with Winnie Mitchell and also denied ever telling anyone that she was 'in trouble' or that he wished he could find a young man to take her away. He alleged that Winnie had told him that she was going to meet a man from Poole and that she had arranged to leave her bicycle in Burton's garden so that he could return it to her mother. He admitted to being surprised to find the bike behind the hayrick.

Asked why he had never mentioned the man from Poole to the police, Burton insisted that Winnie had told him not to say anything.

'If this "man from Poole" had murdered the girl, would you not have liked to see him tried and hanged?' asked Mr Foote for the prosecution.

'I do not know that he did it, sir', replied Burton

In his summing up of the case for the jury, the judge described the murder of Winifred Mitchell as both cruel and deliberate. The accused, he stated, had been most astute in trying to cover up his actions but the judge questioned why not a word had been heard by anyone about a man from Poole until the trial. Had the man from Poole been in the area in the week prior to the murder, digging a grave in the Sovell Plantation? If Burton's story of the man from Poole were true, why had he not told it before?

The jury were absent for just nineteen minutes before returning with a verdict of 'Guilty'. William Walter Burton was sentenced to death.

He was hanged at Dorchester by Thomas Pierrepoint on 24 June 1913, having made a full confession of his guilt before he died. He purported to have been 'proper led away' by Winnie and said that she had 'made him believe all sorts'. The irony of the case was that the post-mortem examination had confirmed that, although Winnie was not a virgin, she was definitely not pregnant. Whether she genuinely believed that she was, or whether her claim to pregnancy was simply a ruse on her part to take her lover away from his wife, will never be known.

Whatever the case, but for the discovery of Winnie's false teeth it is likely that her murder would have remained undiscovered and that her killer would have been free to continue living the life of a respectable pillar of the community.

13

'I AM INNOCENT OF THIS CRIME — ABSOLUTELY'

Tuckton, 1921

Irene May Wilkins was a modest, rather shy spinster who came from a good family. The daughter of a former London barrister, she had reached the age of thirty-one without marrying and, as far as her widowed mother and her three siblings were aware, had no men friends.

During the First World War, she had worked as an inspector with the Army and Navy Canteen Board at a munitions factory in Gretna Green. When the hostilities ended, she worked as a lady cook but, on 20 December 1921, she was between posts and decided to place an advertisement in the Situations Wanted column of the *Morning Post*: 'Lady cook, 31, requires post in a school. Experienced in a school with forty boarders. Disengaged. Salary £65. Miss Irene Wilkins, 21 Thirlmere Road, Streatham SW16.'

No sooner had her advertisement appeared in the newspaper than Irene received a telegram, sent from Boscombe post office near Bournemouth. 'Morning Post. Come immediately 4.30 train Waterloo. Bournmouth [*sic*] Central. Car will meet train. Expence [*sic*] no object. Urgent. Wood, Beech House'.

Irene sent back a telegram confirming that she would attend for an interview and packed an overnight bag containing her nightclothes, a green shantung Dorothy bag, a black and white tartan sponge bag, a hairbrush and comb and some money. However, to the consternation of her mother, brother and two sisters, just after she had left to catch her train, her telegram was returned address unknown.

SHELTERS AND PROMENADE, BOURNEMOUTH.   293

Bournemouth Promenade, 1932.

Their worst fears were realised when they read in the newspaper the following morning that the body of a woman had been found by retired labourer Charles Nicklen in a field in Tuckton, on the outskirts of Bournemouth. The deceased had not yet been identified, but was wearing a gold watch engraved with the initials 'IMW' and had the name 'I Wilkins' marked on some of her underclothes. Irene's brother, Noel, immediately contacted the police in Streatham.

Nicklen had been on his regular morning walk at 7.30 a.m. on 23 December when he had spotted some cows taking an unusual interest in an object in a field. His curiosity aroused, Nicklen went for a closer look and found the woman lying on her back, her legs wide apart and her face covered in blood and bruises. After touching the body to make absolutely sure that the woman was dead, Nicklen hurried to a nearby waterworks, from where the police were called.

Officers arrived at Tuckton before 8 a.m., followed shortly by police surgeon Dr Harold Simmons. They found the woman lying on blood-saturated ground, concealed behind a gorse bush. It appeared that she had been attacked on the gravel path that ran outside the field, since the stones were disturbed as if a struggle had taken place there and a trail of blood led between the path and the body. There were traces of blood on the barbed wire fence enclosing the field, and a woman's umbrella, also bloodstained, lay nearby. Just a few yards away in the road was a brown suede hat trimmed with red ribbons, and in the dirt at the side of the road were clear tyre tracks, which police later determined had been made by a vehicle fitted with Dunlop Magnum tyres.

On initial examination by the doctor, the woman was found to have numerous head wounds varying in severity, which had bled profusely. Rigor mortis was present in her arms and legs and her hands were clenched and stained with blood, as if she had fought hard for her life. Simmons theorised that some of the wounds had been caused by a fist, others by a blunt instrument, such as a hammer, which seemed to have had a projection of some kind or a curved end. He estimated that the woman had been dead for anywhere between five and thirty-six hours.

At a later post-mortem examination, Simmons established that the woman had several skull fractures and that pieces of bone had been driven into her brain. The cause of death was given as shock and blood loss due to severe wounds to the head and face. Her stomach contained approximately two ounces of partially digested blood and little else – she had not eaten for some time. Although her skirts had been lifted, exposing her underwear, there was no physical evidence of a sexual assault, but Simmons was unable to say that this had not been attempted. If the victim had not been sexually assaulted, then it was difficult to imagine a motive for her murder, since she had been carrying nothing worth stealing.

As soon as the police heard from the Wilkins family, they learned of the telegram that had been sent from Boscombe post office. On checking at the post office, they found that two similar telegrams had been sent to different recipients in the few days prior to the murder.

The first, sent on 17 December, was in answer to another advertisement in the *Morning Post*. Like the telegram to Irene Wilkins, the words 'expences' and 'Bournmouth' were mis-spelled. The recipient, Miss Betty Ditmansen of West Hampstead, decided not to follow up on the telegram since she didn't want to work so far away from London. It was probably one of the best decisions she ever made in her life.

View from Boscombe Pier.

The second telegram had been sent on 20 December to a nursing agency that had advertised its services, again in the *Morning Post*. This telegram requested that a nurse be sent urgently to 'Boscombe Grange' and the agency despatched Nurse Burnside in response. On arriving at Bournemouth, the nurse found no car waiting for her as had been promised. She hailed a taxi and was eventually driven to Boscombe Grange in Percy Road, where the occupants professed to have no knowledge of any telegram and no need for the services of a nurse. Having already enquired at numerous nursing homes in the area and several other addresses that included the word Grange, Nurse Burnside was, by now, tired and somewhat confused. The occupants of Boscombe Grange took pity on her and found her a bed for the night and, the following morning, she went to Boscombe post office to try and locate the sender of the telegram.

By an amazing coincidence, Nurse Burnside was actually in the post office at exactly the same time that the man handed over the telegram to be sent to Irene Wilkins. As she tried to unravel the mystery of her telegram, the very person who sent it must have overheard her!

The police were in no doubt that the same person had sent all the telegrams. They questioned the staff at the post office and found one person, counter clerk Alice Waters, who recalled something of the sender. She had been unable to read one of the words on the telegram form, thinking that the word car looked like 'ear'. She had queried the wording and had been corrected by the sender, who, she recalled, had a particularly gruff, husky voice. Acting on her recollections, the police issued a description of a man that they wanted to speak to in connection with the murder. 'Age 28–30; 5ft 6in to 5ft 8in in height; dressed in a chauffeur's hat and overcoat, blue in colour; having the appearance of a chauffeur; uneducated speech.'

Having spoken to railway workers and taxi drivers who had been at the station in Bournemouth at time when Irene Wilkins had expected to have been met, they also put out an appeal for the owners of a dark blue six-cylinder Sunbeam with the letter X in the registration plate and a large grey car with black wings and a Middlesex registration plate to come forward. Another car that they were anxious to trace – which may or may not have been the Sunbeam – bore the registration XE 5086, and another had the numbers 7006, but no index letter or letters were known.

Two taxi drivers both claimed to have seen Irene Wilkins at the station but their accounts differed. Mr Webb remembered Irene wearing a light coloured cloak, while Mr Brown recalled it as being dark purple. Neither description matched the clothes that Irene Wilkins had actually been wearing when she set out for Bournemouth, which were described by her mother as a heavy brown coat, brown suede hat, blue woollen jumper, navy blue skirt and black shoes and stockings

Meanwhile, at an inquest into the death of Irene Wilkins held on 27 December, the jury returned a verdict of wilful murder by person or persons unknown.

The first real breakthrough in the investigation came on 31 December when Benjamin Barnley, an unemployed groom, was walking on Canford Cliffs, about eight miles from where Irene's body had been discovered, and spotted a folded woman's nightdress on the ground. When he looked more closely, he found an attaché case, an empty purse and

Canford Cliffs, 1933.

assorted personal possessions concealed under a rhododendron bush. The effects included an envelope containing an Army testimonial for Irene May Wilkins and the telegram she had been sent summoning her to Bournemouth. Realising the significance of his find, Barnley went straight to the police station. The items were damp and stained with mildew and had obviously been there for some time. Surprisingly, Barnley had walked the same path six times a day for the previous nine days and had not previously noticed anything.

On the same day, Superintendent Shadrach Garrett of the Hampshire Police issued a new appeal for information. Accusing the public of apathy, Garrett said that the police had been unable to trace any of Irene Wilkins's movements after she left home. Reported sightings of a woman matching her description seen at Bournemouth station were conflicting and not conclusive. They were interested in details of any cars seen at the station on 22 December and were now also seeking the driver of a two-seater car seen parked with its headlights on near the woods where the attaché case had been found.

It was estimated that between twelve and fifteen cars had been at the station at the crucial time and, so far, only six owners or drivers had come forward. Of particular interest were the large six-cylinder Sunbeam, another large six-cylinder car of unknown manufacture and also some two-seaters. Eventually, the police decided to examine all the cars in the district, asking owners, drivers and chauffeurs to submit their cars for examination. As tyre marks had been found near to where Irene's body had been dumped, they naturally paid particular attention to the tyres. At the same time, the police took the decision to publish a copy of the telegram in the local and national newspapers, in the hope that someone may recognise the handwriting.

One man who was interviewed at the time was Thomas Henry Allaway, a thirty-six-year-old chauffeur employed by a Mr Arthur Sutton, who was then resident at the Carlton Hotel, Bournemouth. Allaway lived with his wife and three-year-old daughter in Haviland Road, Boscombe, and routinely garaged his employer's car at Portman Mews Garage, Boscombe.

Allaway was seen by police on 7 January, and his employer's car, a Mercedes with the registration number LK 7405, was inspected. The car's front tyres were both Dunlop Magnums, while the rear tyres were one Dunlop Magnum and one Michelin. Allaway told the police that the car tyres had not been changed since 22 December.

Nothing about the car excited suspicion and Allaway was able to account for his movements on the evening of 22 December. He was asked to write copies of the decoy telegrams, but his handwriting differed from that on the originals.

The case dragged on unsolved, although the police continued to make exhaustive enquiries, staging a reconstruction and even apparently calling on the services of psychics and mediums. With no further leads, in April 1922, Superintendent Garrett ordered a full review of all the documentation pertaining to the enquiry, which by that time numbered in excess of 20,000 items.

Among the statements revisited were two made by engineer Frank Humphris. Superintendent Garrett had read the first statement, made within forty-eight hours, in which Humphris described alighting from the 4.30 p.m. train at Bournemouth and seeing a woman resembling the description of Irene Wilkins being driven off in a car by a man. Humphris had given a good description of both the man and the car.

On the morning of 4 January, Humphris had again presented himself at the police station to say that he had just seen the same man and car at the station. This time he had the presence of mind to write down the car's make and registration number. It was the Mercedes LK 7405, registered to Allaway's employer.

Allaway was interviewed as a consequence of this statement, but incredibly the evidence linking him and his car to Bournemouth station at the crucial time was misplaced and consequently Garrett didn't see it until the third week in April.

Over the course of the investigations, various pieces of information about Allaway had reached the police. Walter Randall, who garaged his vehicle in the same place as Allaway's, claimed that the Mercedes was not in its usual place at the time of the murder and that Allaway had changed one of the car's tyres on 24 December, just two days later. Allaway's employer's son lived at a place called 'Beech Hurst', which was a similar name to the 'Beech House' used in the telegram sent to Nurse Burnside. And finally, his employer's sister-in-law lived just a few yards from the spot where Irene's case had been found and, on 23 December, Allaway had driven Mrs Sutton there to take tea, waiting outside in the car for her for more than an hour.

While these snippets of information about Allaway were purely circumstantial evidence, Humphris's second statement seemed to link him to Bournemouth station and to a woman matching the description of Irene Wilkins. Allaway was promptly elevated to the top of the list of suspects.

Allaway and his family had recently moved house from Haviland Road to a flat in Windsor Road, Boscombe. He must have got wind of the renewed police interest in him as he began to make preparations to flee the area. On 20 April, he stole his employer's chequebook and forged Sutton's signature, obtaining more than £20 from local traders who knew him as Sutton's chauffeur. He sent his wife and child to her parents' home in Reading and he himself travelled to North London, using the alias Mr T. Cook.

The theft of the cheques was reported to the police on 22 April and Inspector Brewer was sent to London to arrest Allaway for forgery. However, Brewer was unable to locate his quarry and accordingly a watch was placed on the Reading home of Allaway's in-laws. On the evening of 28 April, Allaway was spotted arriving at Reading but, as the police moved in to apprehend him, he ran off. A passer-by saw the resulting chase and stuck out a foot, sending Allaway sprawling, thus allowing the police to capture him.

Charged with forgery, Allaway was detained at Reading until Superintendent Garrett arrived to collect him and escort him back to Bournemouth. While in Reading, Garrett visited Mrs May Allaway to obtain some samples of her husband's writing. With her permission, police later took possession of seven postcards from the flat in Boscombe that her husband had sent to her in the past. These were sent to a handwriting expert in London, Mr Gerald Guerin, along with the decoy telegrams and some betting slips found in Allaway's pockets on his arrest. Guerin was certain that the postcards and telegrams were written by the same hand and, having examined the betting slips, he also pointed out that the chauffeur had changed his handwriting style since 22 December.

Thomas Allaway arrives at Winchester Assizes for his trial. (Daily Echo, Bournemouth)

Back in Bournemouth, Allaway was placed in an identity parade with several other men dressed in chauffeur's uniforms. Witnesses, including Mr Humphris and post office clerk Alice Waters, picked him out of the line up immediately, while newsagent Albert Samways had no hesitation in identifying him as one of two men who had purchased a *Morning Post* newspaper from him on 22 December. One of the other members of the identity parade was very similar in physical appearance to Allaway and some witnesses initially picked out the look-alike. Most seemed to realise that they had made an error and asked for a second look, this time choosing Allaway.

On 6 May, Thomas Henry Allaway was formally charged with the murder of Irene Wilkins. Asserting his innocence, he asked police for a pen and paper so that he might write a statement. The resulting document was riddled with spelling mistakes and the handwriting was seen to change in style from upright to the right-handed slope of the telegrams.

After magistrates at Bournemouth Police Court heard the case, they committed Allaway to stand trial at the next Hampshire Assizes. The proceedings opened at Winchester Castle on 3 July 1922, with Mr Justice Avory presiding. Mr Thomas Inskip KC MP led the case for the prosecution, while Mr A.C. Fox Davies defended.

No less than forty-three witnesses were called for the prosecution while only eighteen appeared for the defence, including Allaway himself. The accused first denied having written any of the telegrams. The postcards to his wife, written while he was serving in Germany with a motor ambulance convoy in 1918, had been penned for him by another man, after he had sprained his wrist starting an engine. He also denied having changed his handwriting after the murder and was most emphatic in stating that he had not killed Irene Wilkins, saying that, at the time of her murder, he had been in a Working Men's Club and later the Salisbury Hotel. Yet, in the course of giving evidence, Allaway also proved himself to be poor at spelling. Asked by the judge to spell the word pleasant, he immediately replied that it was spelled like the word present. The telegram to Nurse Burnside had requested a 'plesent [*sic*] companion'.

The purpose of most of the defence witnesses was to support Allaway's alibi. A Mrs Dundee confirmed that she had seen Allaway in Boscombe at 8 p.m. on the night of the murder. She was certain of the date, because she had been going to the Hippodrome to see a performance. Several witnesses recalled seeing the defendant in the Conservative Club and several more remembered that he was in the Salisbury Hotel from 8.05 p.m. to 9.55 p.m. Charles Barrett, the owner of the Portman Mews garage, stated that he had locked the Mercedes in the garage at about 6.15 p.m. Barrett said that he had the only key to the premises, although this particular evidence was disproved as a copied key had been found at the Allaway's home. Taxi driver George Troke also testified that Mr Sutton's car had been locked in the garage at the time of the murder. However, although all of these witnesses initially appeared certain of the truth of their statements, it became evident during cross-examination that most were confusing dates and times.

Postman Arthur Elkins was a much more credible witness for the defence. On the night of the murder, he had moved his goats near the field at Tuckton in which the body was found. At 8.15 p.m., he had seen a car with dimmed headlights parked near to the scene of the crime and the car was still there when he returned about half an hour later. His hat had blown off and landed very close to the car, so he had got a good look at and described it as small, dark and looking like a taxi cab, nothing like the large Mercedes driven by Allaway.

May Allaway had stood by her husband all along and now she too gave evidence in his defence. On the night of the murder, she stated that she had left him at the Conservative Club at about 7 p.m. and gone to the cinema alone. She had met her husband by prior arrangement at the Salisbury Hotel, finding him already there when she arrived at 8.50 p.m. His appearance and behaviour that evening was completely normal and she had noticed no stains on his clothing and had seen no changes in him since the murder. She also stated that a screw-hammer and spanner found at Allaway's home, and thought to be the murder weapons, had been stored in London and had not arrived in Boscombe until the end of January.

The defence witnesses failed to convince the jury, who also managed to ignore a passionate display by Allaway's mother who, during the course of the Judge's summing up, suddenly fell to her knees in prayer. After deliberating for an hour, they returned a verdict of 'Guilty'.

Asked by the clerk of the court if he had anything to say as to why he should not receive judgement of death, Allaway was so shocked at the verdict that he didn't hear the question and had to ask for it to be repeated. When it was, he responded, 'I am innocent of this crime – absolutely'.

His declaration of innocence had no effect on the judge who promptly sentenced him to death for what he described as 'this foul and brutal murder'. As Allaway left the court, he suddenly glared at the judge with what one observer described as 'a look of concentrated malevolence, which revealed for a fraction of time the brutal soul within him.'

An appeal was immediately lodged but it proved unsuccessful and Allaway's execution was scheduled for 19 August 1922. Shortly before his execution, he apparently made a full confession of his guilt to the prison governor, although when visited by his wife and brother, just hours later, he reverted to claiming his innocence.

John Ellis carried out the execution at Winchester and it was not the most efficient execution of his career, since the noose slipped and, rather than dying from a broken neck, Allaway died from strangulation, his death taking a couple of minutes rather than occurring instantaneously. He died without revealing his motive for the murder.

[Note: In various contemporary accounts of the murder, the man who found Irene Wilkins's body is alternatively named Octavius Nicklen or Charles Nicklen. The finder of her attaché case is named as either Benjamin Barnley or Benjamin Barnby. Engineer Frank Humphris is also referred to as Humphries.]

14

'YOU WOULDN'T CHEAT ME, WOULD YOU?'

Poole, 1925

It was perhaps a measure of the unhappiness of Frederick Young's home life that a stay in the Royal Victoria Hospital in Bournemouth with an injured hand seemed to him like a relaxing holiday. Young, aged forty-six, lived cheerlessly in Francis Road, Branksome, with a wife who was seriously mentally ill and their one son, Alfred, who worked as an errand boy. Yet a break from his work and his clinically insane wife were not the only attractions of the hospital stay for Young – the main highlight was a shapely twenty-one-year-old nurse, Flossie Davies.

Flossie had recently moved to Bournemouth from her native Wales to make a new start, having been jilted by the love of her life. Hence, she was still new to the area and rather lonely and, seeing that Fred Young never received any visitors, she made a special effort to be nice to him. Before long, she was visiting him on her days off. To Flossie, there was something reassuringly safe about Young, who was more than twice her age. Soon, she found herself falling in love with him and offering to live with him when he left hospital.

With his crippled hand preventing him from working, Young took her up on her offer without hesitation. To his neighbours, it was a perfectly respectable arrangement – Young had simply employed a nurse to look after his sick wife. To his son, Alfred, the arrangement was not as respectable as it might outwardly seem, since his Dad and his new 'Auntie Flossie' were sharing a bedroom. Flossie would not immediately agree to share Fred's bed, while his wife slept alone in a different room. However, Fred pleaded and cajoled and swore undying love for her in order to persuade her, and eventually she

Francis Road, Poole, 2008. (© N. Sly)

Royal Victoria and West Hampshire Hospital, Boscombe, 1930s.

capitulated for fear of losing him. Yet although she and Fred became lovers, Flossie's strict religious upbringing meant that, even while they shared the most intimate moments, she could not forgive herself for committing what she saw as a terrible sin.

Before too long, the inevitable happened and Flossie fell pregnant. Fred's reaction to hearing the news was to bury his head in his hands and exclaim, 'Oh, my God!'

'God won't help us. We are sinners', Flossie told him.

While Fred went out for a walk to contemplate the probable consequences of his sinning, Flossie sat down and wrote a long, dramatic letter to Alfred, the boyfriend who had jilted her. Calling him 'the only person I ever loved', she explained to him that she had tried to commit suicide once before, after he had left her, by taking what she thought was a fatal dose of morphine, mixed with a spoonful of jam. Now, she told him that the very thought of the degraded life that she was living at the moment made her feel sick. She was going to end it all and she thought that 'Uncle Fred' would probably choose to come with her, since he was fed up with life and in constant pain. Telling Alfred that she wanted him to have her fountain pen to remember her by, she ended the letter 'Your Flossie XXX'. She then added a postscript telling him that he would only receive the letter after she was dead and asking him to forgive her. 'It is so much easier to die than to live', she wrote. 'Oh, sweetheart of my youth and womanhood, what have I done to deserve all I had to go through?' she asked, ending, 'Goodbye, dear. I am almost heartbroken now'.

When Fred returned from his walk, Flossie spurned all physical contact with him. 'How much do you love me?' she asked him. 'Could you live without me? If I died, would you want to go on living?'

'Of course not', replied Fred, his mind almost certainly more focused on persuading her to let him back into their shared bed than on the questions she was asking. It was then that Flossie put forward the idea of a suicide pact between them.

Sensing her distress, Fred felt that he had no choice but to agree, thinking that he could probably talk her round later. He obviously gave the right answer because only now was Fred permitted to make love to Flossie again. Before they fell asleep, Flossie had just one more question for him.

'You wouldn't cheat me, would you?'

Fred misunderstood the question, thinking that she was referring to physical infidelity, but Flossie quickly corrected him. 'Our suicide pact – you wouldn't have me go and then not follow, would you? I'd be so terrified going alone.'

Fred promised and, reassured, Flossie soon fell asleep. Fred, however, lay awake for hours on end, listening to her steady breathing and thinking about what he had to do next.

Early the next morning, 11 August 1925, Young's son Alfred was awakened by the sound of somebody shouting his name. He got up and went along the landing, seeing his father standing in the doorway of the bedroom he shared with 'Aunt Flossie'. As Alfred approached, he caught a glimpse of 'Aunt Flossie' through the open door. She was sprawled on the bed, her head almost detached from her body and the whole room seemed almost awash with her blood.

'Your Aunt Flossie is dead', his father explained. 'Go to the Bourne Valley police station and bring the police back here.'

Alfred ran to the police station as fast as he could, but it was only 6.30 a.m. and the doors were still locked. Not knowing what to do next, he ran back to the house, finding the bedroom door now closed and his father standing calmly in front of it.

'Are they coming?' asked Fred.

Alfred explained that the police station was still closed and he sent for the doctor instead. However, when he reached Dr Montgomery's house, he was to learn that the doctor was already out on a call. Leaving a message for the doctor to come as soon as he was able, Alfred turned for home again.

It seemed to Alfred as if his father desperately wanted him to fetch someone and now, for the second time, he had failed. Before going home, he made the decision to call on one of the neighbours for help and so he stopped at the house of Mr and Mrs Allen, who lived a couple of houses away in Francis Road, banging loudly on the door until a sleepy Mr Allen answered.

Mr and Mrs Allen were naturally shaken as young Alfred babbled on about 'Aunt Flossie' being dead. They asked him in, and Mrs Allen made him a cup of tea while her husband got dressed. If the truth were told, Mr Allen was none too keen to see what, from Alfred's garbled description, sounded like a very bloody scene and tried to delay things as long as he could. As a result, it was nearly 8 a.m. before the distressed boy finally managed to persuade Mr Allen to go back home with him.

Reluctantly, Mr Allen allowed the boy to pull him to the house next door but one and push him through the front door and upstairs. The squeamish Mr Allen took just one glance at Fred Young, who was standing in exactly the same place that Alfred had left him, before screaming 'Bloody Hell!' and bolting. He left the house as fast as he could, announcing his intention to fetch the police. For Fred Young now had a gaping wound in his throat, that pumped out jets of bright red blood with every beat of his heart.

In the event, it was not the police who were first on the scene, but a doctor, Dr Stanley Rowbottom. After giving Fred Young what first aid he could, he pushed open the door to the bedroom, realising immediately that there was nothing he could do for Flossie, who, he estimated, had been dead for at least two hours.

The police soon arrived and Young was rushed to Poole hospital with a police escort. Although his vocal chords had been severed, leaving him unable to speak, he was well enough to write and sign a statement in which he denied having any part in the death of Flossie Davies, saying that he had woken that morning to find her dead in bed beside him.

The carnage in the bedroom at 12 Francis Road told a very different story. A razor, with several pieces of its blade missing was found embedded in the blood on the bedroom floor. So deep was the wound to her throat, which had almost completely decapitated her, that the missing pieces of steel from the blade were buried in Flossie's backbone. Almost everything in the bedroom was soaked with blood. However, Flossie's hands were completely clean, indicating that she hadn't cut her own throat but that somebody had cut it for her.

Young was promptly charged with the wilful murder of Flossie Davies.

He appeared in court at Dorchester before Judge Rowlatt, looking weak and ill, with his throat heavily bandaged, still maintaining that Flossie Davies had committed suicide as her part of a pact between them. His barrister, Ernest Charles KC, tried to tell the court that Young was so severely disabled as a result of injury that his left hand and arm were completely useless, and a one-armed man would not have been able to hold Flossie and simultaneously cut her throat.

'It takes but one hand to hold a razor', suggested the counsel for the prosecution, J.D. Roberts.

'Quite so', agreed Charles, 'if the victim obligingly remains still.'

'Or is asleep', countered Roberts, acidly.

Fred Young was called to give evidence, but, since he could only speak in a husky whisper, he could barely make himself heard in the courtroom. Dr Rowbottom, in court to give his own evidence, offered to sit beside him and repeat every word that he said.

Via Rowbottom, Young told the court that he had woken up in the early hours of the morning to find Flossie Davies lighting a candle and putting on her dressing gown, with the intention of going down to the kitchen for an apple and a glass of lemonade. He had offered to fetch them for her and, when he returned to the bedroom, had found Flossie in the act of cutting her own throat.

According to Young, the razor belonged not to him, but to Flossie herself. She regularly used it to shave her own neck. In addition, Flossie was an unstable person whom he had once caught taking morphine, which she stashed in her handbag. Young denied ever having discussed suicide with Flossie Davies, saying that he did not offer to cut her throat and he did not want to get rid of her.

In his summary of the case, Mr Justice Rowlatt was very scathing about what he described as the 'loose talk and gush' surrounding the suicide pact between Young and Davies. It was not at all a bad way to commit a murder, he told the jury, to make an agreement of this sort and, while the other person committed suicide, for the murderer not to follow suit. Nevertheless, he accepted that the letter to Flossie's previous boyfriend indicated that there had been some talk of a pact between the lovers, but it did not indicate that any firm agreement to proceed had been made. It was not his job to disprove, he concluded, but the prosecution's job to prove beyond all reasonable doubt that the girl had her throat cut at the hand of Young. The jury must decide between straight murder and no murder at all in reaching their verdict.

The jury took just over an hour to choose 'straight murder' and Young was sentenced to death. Still a very sick man, he was taken from court to the infirmary at Dorchester Prison, where doctors began the difficult task of keeping him alive until his execution.

The day before he was scheduled to die, Young began to complain of severe pain. The prison doctor, Dr Francis Nash-Wortham, was called to his bedside where an examination showed that very little air was getting into his lungs. Nash-Wortham prescribed an ounce of brandy every quarter of an hour, in the hope of easing the spasms in Young's larynx. He then went off to see other patients, returning three hours later to find that

Young's condition had worsened considerably. Now in a collapsed state, the prisoner was pale and clammy, his pulse weak and feeble.

Nash-Wortham was then called to deal with another crisis. Some time later, prison officer Henry Moore saw that Young was becoming weaker still and summoned Dr Mann, Nash-Wortham's partner and locum. By the time Mann arrived five minutes later, Young had died.

A post-mortem examination was carried out by Nash-Wortham and an inquest held into his death before Major G.G.H. Symes, the deputy coroner for South Dorset. There, Nash-Wortham revealed that Young's vocal passages were so obstructed by scar tissue that, instead of being the diameter of a pencil as they would normally be, they would now scarcely allow the passage of a pin head. Young was also suffering from aortic disease of the heart and both of his lungs had partially collapsed, putting the diseased heart under an enormous strain.

The coroner's jury agreed to waive their fees, asking that the money be forwarded to Young's son, Alfred. Young's relatives were given permission to collect his body and held a simple funeral for him, attended by only the presiding vicar and Young's father, brother, and sister-in-law. Frederick Arthur Young may have cheated the hangman but, in the end, he had not cheated Flossie Davies.

15

'MY HEAD FEELS AWFUL QUEER'

Bournemouth, 1926

The Wright family came to live in Bournemouth in 1923. Some believed that they had come from Manchester, but head of the family Robert, who was by then in his early sixties, did not indulge in gossip, so very little information could be elicited about his previous life. His wife, Beatrice, a much younger woman, then in her late twenties, was equally tight-lipped.

The couple, together with their infant daughter, Marjory, found lodgings at St Swithun's Road, Bournemouth, in a house that was divided into two flats. The Wright family lived in the top floor flat, while their landlady occupied the flat below. As the months passed, it became evident to their landlady that Robert was very much a family man, who was devoted to his wife and child. A lifelong teetotaller, he quickly found well-paid work as a carpenter and spent his evenings after work mending boots and shoes to bring in a little extra income. He professed himself proud to be using his hands to work in the same profession as 'our Lord Jesus Christ'.

One day, while Robert was at work, his landlady got chatting to Beatrice, remarking casually that her husband seemed like a man who had 'known much better things'. The normally reticent Beatrice found herself opening up to their kind landlady, confiding that Robert was very well educated and had travelled the world while in the Army. She also revealed that he had a brother who held a position of some importance in Argentina.

After twelve months of living happily in St Swithun's Road, their landlady hesitantly approached Robert with some bad news. She had to move house but, if they wanted, there was plenty of room for the family at her new home, including the baby that

St Swithun's Road, Bournemouth, 2008. (© N. Sly)

Beatrice was expecting. Robert and Beatrice were delighted and began to prepare for the move. However, their hopes of continuing with their happy domestic arrangements were suddenly and unexpectedly dashed when the firm that Robert worked for announced that they were to close.

Without a job and a regular wage, Robert did not feel comfortable impinging on their landlady's goodwill and, although she pleaded with them to move, saying that she was happy to wait for the rent until Robert found another job, the proud, independent Robert just could not bring himself to be indebted to her.

When the house at St Swithun's Road was sold up, he moved his family into another rented home in Bournemouth Road, Parkstone. A second daughter, Amy Violet, arrived shortly afterwards. Robert spent his days walking the streets looking for work and the evenings playing with his children or sitting quietly with Beatrice in their sparsely furnished rooms. He continued to promise Beatrice that, one day, things would get better and that they would have a house of their own, rather than paying rent to other people.

The Wright family was in dire financial straits but, in August 1925, things gradually began to improve. It was then that Beatrice was reunited with Frederick Giles, her long-estranged father, who was finally introduced to the son-in-law and grandchildren he had never met. When father and daughter had a few moments alone together, Fred asked Beatrice if she was happy. 'Life has been tough of late, Dad', Beatrice admitted, but was quick to add that she had a really good man who couldn't do enough for her and her children.

Constitution Hill, Parkstone.

Then, just a short while later, Robert Wright finally found a new job, starting work for local builder Mr Hoare on 17 August.

Wright was a resounding success at his new place of work. According to his foreman, William Howe, he was a working machine, ready to tackle any job given to him, no matter how hard or how unpleasant. When Mr Hoare asked if Wright were worth the money he was being paid, Howe told him that he could pay him ten times his current wage and still be getting a bargain. Yet, no matter how impressed he was with his employee, Hoare could only afford to pay him a basic wage and, after Wright's period of unemployment, during which the couple had found themselves with outstanding accounts to tradespeople, he found himself gradually slipping further and further into debt.

Matters came to a head when young Amy Violet fell ill. The only food that Beatrice could afford to feed her children was the cheapest possible available and it was far from a healthy, nutritious diet. Now, Amy Violet lay in her makeshift cot, feverish and sick, and, having already pawned all but the bare necessities, her parents were too poor to send for a doctor to treat her.

Both parents took it in turns to sit up all night with their poorly daughter, trying their hardest to keep her warm and comfortable, with Robert always putting in a full day's work despite his lack of sleep. However, the hard work and exhaustion began to tell on him and he went down with a bad attack of influenza. He refused to let his illness prevent him from working, telling Beatrice that it was just a cold and continuing to cycle to his job every day as he had always done.

Beatrice was now unable to obtain even milk to feed her children, since her account with the dairy was long overdue. Her family was kept alive only by the kindness and compassion of Mr Chalkley, the milkman, who continued to allow her to have a little milk every day, even though she had already run up a substantial bill.

Robert's employer and work colleagues noticed that he was looking pale and worn, even though he refused to let his work rate slip because of his illness. He allowed himself one day off work on Christmas Day – a day like every other in the Wright household, since no money could be found for any form of celebration – then he resumed working, still feeling weak and complaining privately to Beatrice, 'My head feels awful queer'.

Somehow, Beatrice managed to scrape up enough money to pay off some of the arrears she owed for milk, but that left her short of money to pay Mr Jewlett, the coal merchant, and soon he too was refusing to deliver. Jewlett sympathised with the Wrights but he had a business to run. Eventually, he agreed that, although he wouldn't allow the family to have any more coal, he would also not pressure them for payment of the outstanding bill for the two hundredweight of coal that they had already received and not yet paid for.

On New Year's Day 1926, Robert Wright dropped a bombshell. He went to see Bill Howe, his foreman at Hoare's and handed in his notice with immediate effect. Howe asked him if he had another job to go to, but the taciturn Wright would only say that he had, without offering any more details.

Beatrice was shocked and horrified when he broke the news of his unemployment to her that evening, even more so when Robert told her that he had resigned rather than been laid off or sacked. However, Robert assured her that he had a plan and, trusting his judgement, she didn't push for more information, accepting that he would tell her when he was good and ready.

It was January. The weather was cold and wintry and Robert and Beatrice were living in rented accommodation without the means to heat it and too poor to buy food for themselves or their two daughters. As before, it was Chalkley the milkman who came to the rescue. He had become very fond of the two little girls, Marjory, now three years old and Amy Violet, aged twenty-two months, and, unpaid bills or not, he couldn't bear the thought of the children starving for want of milk. Hence he continued to ladle milk into Mrs Wright's jug each day and to accept her constant promises that he would be paid in full very soon.

Wright left the house briefly on 5 January to collect his tools from Hoare's. Apart from this one short excursion, none of the Wright family was seen outside the house and, when tradesmen to whom they owed money knocked on the door, their knocks went unanswered.

On 26 January 1926, Chalkley again decided to try and collect some of his outstanding bill. He knocked on the door of the Wright home and was not particularly surprised to receive no reply. However, as he was leaving, he happened to glance down and noticed that the jug of milk that he had filled for Beatrice the previous day was still standing untouched on the doorstep. Recognising that something was seriously wrong, he immediately went to the police and at half-past two in the afternoon; PC Lake arrived in Bournemouth Road to investigate.

He managed to gain entrance to the property by a broken pane of glass in the back door. The blinds were drawn and the house was in partial darkness. Lake made his way carefully across the deserted living room and upstairs to the bedroom, where the blinds were also drawn closed. As he opened the bedroom door, Lake was aware of something heavy falling against his foot. As his eyes gradually became accustomed to the dim light, he realised that he was facing a pair of double beds and in those beds lay all four members of the Wright family, all of them dead. Averting his eyes immediately from the gruesome scene of carnage that faced him, Lake looked down to see what had fallen against his foot. It was a heavily bloodstained axe.

Lake rushed to summon assistance and before long reinforcements arrived in the form of PC Trevis and Dr Patterson. Struggling to keep his balance on a floor slippery with spilled blood, Patterson ascertained that Beatrice and the two girls had been almost decapitated by the axe. Robert, dressed in just trousers and stockinged feet, lay across the foot of the bed, a razor at his side, with several gaping cuts across his throat. All had been dead for more than twenty-four hours.

Police began a search of the house and found a bloodstained collar downstairs on the kitchen table. On the mantelpiece lay a shilling and two sixpences and a holdall was found that contained little else but Robert Wright's insurance card. Apart from that, the house was woefully bare, its occupants having pawned almost everything they owned in a desperate struggle to survive. Neighbours were interviewed and, although they could offer little insight into the tragedy, one did recall hearing a scream the previous Sunday, which appeared to come from the direction of the Wright's house.

An inquest was opened into the deaths of Robert, Beatrice and the two little girls who had been formally identified by Beatrice's father, Mr Giles. Mr Hatton Budge, the coroner, professed himself to be mystified at the circumstances regarding the family's deaths. Nobody could be found who knew why the Wrights had moved to Bournemouth from Manchester – if indeed it had been Manchester they had come from. Mr Giles told the coroner that he could only think of one person – Robert's brother – who might be able to shed some light on the Wright's recent life. However, he did not know the brother's name or address, beyond thinking that he was living somewhere in New Jersey, America.

Dr Patterson had conducted post-mortem examinations on all four bodies and had determined that death for the two girls had at least been relatively quick. Both were dressed in their nightclothes and lay as if sleeping, one still clutching a ragged doll. The cause of death for Marjory and Amy Violet was given as the severing of their spinal cords by injuries to the back of the neck, caused by the axe found in the bedroom.

For Beatrice Wright, the end had been less swift. The fact that one of her neighbours had heard a scream seemed to suggest that she had been awake when she was attacked and received a large wound to the back of her head. When found, she was sitting partially upright, rather than lying down and Patterson believed that she had been aware of what was about to happen and had begun to take evasive action. Robert, Patterson stated, had cut his own throat with a razor.

With so little known about the Wright family and their circumstances, all the coroner's jury could do was to return a verdict that Robert Percy Wright had killed his wife and children and then himself while temporarily insane.

A funeral was held for the family and, unusually, Robert was allowed to be buried with his family. (Frequently those who committed suicide were not permitted a burial in consecrated ground.) Their funeral attracted large crowds, but among those were very few people who had actually known the Wright family in life. Even Mr Giles, the only relative to attend, was a virtual stranger, having only recently met the daughter from whom he had been estranged for many years.

The family were buried in a double grave in Parkstone cemetery. Unsurprisingly, no form of headstone has ever been erected to mark their final resting place or their memory.

16

'I WILL HAVE YOU ALL, ONE AT A TIME'

Wimborne, 1930

Captain Frank Hawkeswood Burdett moved to Wimborne shortly after the end of the First World War, to a bungalow that he named Handicraft House, probably because of his love of leather craft. His tooled leather products were of the highest quality and Burdett frequently exhibited his work in nearby Bournemouth and Dorchester.

There were two sides to Captain Burdett. He was a community-minded man, who worked tirelessly in local politics and was prepared to knuckle down and organise events in the area, while other people preferred to watch from the sidelines and enjoy the fruits of his efforts without getting involved in any of the work. However, his other side was less appealing – Frank Burdett was a braggart and a liar, who embroidered his rather lonely life with tall tales and boasts. For instance, when complimented on his leatherwork, he insisted that members of the royal family were regular purchasers of his handiwork, deftly changing the subject when he was pumped for more details of his royal patrons. Since he was never prepared to discuss his private life prior to arriving in Wimborne, many of the townspeople doubted his military service and thus his entitlement to call himself Captain.

For the most part, Burdett was a quiet, unassuming and rather likeable man, but his increasingly frequent bouts of arrogance and boasting were gradually beginning to alienate the people of Wimborne, to whom he soon became a bit of a joke.

The last straw came with a confrontation at his local pub, the Horns Inn. Normally, Frank would sit quietly in a corner, enjoying a drink and a chat with the regulars. However, one day, he elected instead to stand at the bar all evening, loudly telling the landlord how he should be conducting his business. Eventually, the landlord grew so irritated by the unwelcome advice, that he threw Burdett out and banned him from ever drinking in the pub again. This incident marked a turning point for Burdett, as the locals sided with the landlord and Burdett found himself ostracised.

Only one family stood by him. Thomas Holloway of Walford Farm was outraged at the treatment of his near neighbour by the townspeople. Holloway told his wife that the very least people could do was treat Burdett like a human being, and decided to pave the way to fostering better relations between the Captain and the locals by inviting Burdett to dine at his house.

Thus, social pariah Burdett came to be eating supper with the Holloway family, Thomas, his wife Louise, their four adult sons, Alfred, Ernest, Maurice and Archibald, and their eighteen-year-old daughter Beatrix, known as Trixie. At first, the conversation around the dinner table was stilted and not helped by the fact that, when asked by the Holloways about his experiences in the Army, Burdett neatly sidestepped the question, claiming that talk of his war experiences would bore the young people. Instead, he changed the subject, commiserating with the family on the recent death of their eldest daughter. Thomas Holloway, anxious that his wife should not be upset, quickly interjected to tell his guest about the family's other two sons. Burdett's military career was soon forgotten, to the slight annoyance of Thomas Holloway, who had hoped to be able to put an end to the rumours circulating around Wimborne about Captain Burdett's status.

Still, the evening passed pleasantly enough and the Holloways found Burdett a charming and interesting guest. So much so, that he was invited back again and again. Although he continued to be reticent about speaking of his past, managing to change the subject whenever it looked like becoming the topic of conversation, Burdett was only too ready to talk about his business, so much so that young Trixie expressed an interest in seeing some of his crafts.

Burdett immediately promised to bring some with him on his next visit, then an even better idea occurred to him – perhaps Trixie would like to visit his bungalow to watch how the work was done as well as see the finished articles?

Trixie was allowed to visit Handicraft House and, following her visit, became something of a favourite of the Captain's. At future suppers at Walsford Farm, Burdett paid ever more attention to her, neglecting the other members of the family. Although it was obvious to the Holloways that their guest was slowly distancing himself from them, they were too polite to say anything, until Trixie herself brought matters to a head by announcing to her mother that she and Captain Burdett were in love and intended to get married.

The Holloways were distraught. Captain Burdett was more than three times Trixie's age and old enough to be her grandfather. Thomas Holloway raged, Louise begged and Trixie's brothers pleaded with her to reconsider, but Trixie was beyond listening to reason or commonsense. As the arguments about her future marriage reached a climax, she walked out of the farmhouse in a temper and went to live with Burdett.

In the first half of the twentieth century, a respectable unmarried couple living together as man and wife was almost unheard of. Thomas Holloway not only forbade the rest of his family to speak to Burdett again, but he attempted to thwart his daughter's plans by taking out a charge against Burdett for Trixie's abduction. However, Trixie had made her own application to the court for permission to marry Frank Burdett without her parents' consent.

The Square, Wimborne, 1930s.

The situation was at stalemate when Louise Holloway suggested a compromise. She reasoned that Trixie would never willingly give up her boyfriend and felt that it was better for the Holloways to give their consent to the marriage rather than suffer the shame and disgrace of their daughter 'living in sin'. Thomas Holloway was initially furious about the idea of the marriage taking place, but when he had calmed down a little, he saw the sense in his wife's proposition and went to the magistrates to withdraw his charge. Trixie became Mrs Frank Burdett on 28 May 1930. Hers was not the elaborate wedding of every young girl's dreams. Instead, it was a simple ceremony at Wimborne Register Office, with only the necessary officials and witnesses in attendance. The Holloways may have given their consent to the marriage, but they had not given their blessing and none of the family were present.

Although very much in love, the couple's married life did not get off to the best of starts. Captain Burdett was in dire financial straits, a fact he had kept from his young bride. Wracking his brains to think of a way in which to improve their finances, Burdett came up with a scheme to obtain funds to benefit ex-servicemen, appealing for donations in a London newspaper. However, since the newspaper required evidence that the money was to be used as Burdett said it would be – and since Burdett was likely to be the only ex-serviceman actually benefiting – the scheme never got off the ground. Eventually, Burdett was forced to go cap in hand to the one place where he knew there was money – Walsford Farm.

Having engineered an 'accidental' meeting with Maurice Holloway in a lane near the farm, Burdett feigned surprise when Maurice blanked him completely. Burdett suggested that, now the two men were brothers-in-law, they should put aside their differences for Trixie's sake, but Maurice was having none of it. When Burdett went on to ask him for a small loan, Maurice accused him of crawling to him like a coward, as he must have done during the war.

Enraged by the insult, Burdett lost his temper and began to bluster about how Maurice should be horsewhipped for his insolence. He went on to tell Maurice that, if he knew what was good for him, he would hand over some money immediately.

Maurice's response was to swing his fist at Burdett, landing a punch on his jaw that sent him sprawling onto the muddy lane. As Maurice walked away without a backward glance, Burdett was forced to pick himself up and go home to his wife empty-handed.

Trixie knew nothing of the couple's poverty, although she was about to find out. She was shopping in Wimborne when the shopkeeper hesitantly suggested that she should settle her outstanding account. Trixie discovered that Frank had been booking items from several local shopkeepers in her name, probably under the impression that she would be able to obtain money from her father to pay the bills. She made up her mind to speak to her husband but, when she arrived home, she found Frank in a deep depression and was afraid of upsetting him further.

Hence, she said nothing but instead set about preparing supper while Burdett, who told her that he had a headache, went out for a walk on the pretext of getting some fresh air. Instead, he went straight to Walsford Farm, this time seeking out Thomas Holloway and begging him for a loan. Holloway ignored him completely, refusing to even acknowledge his presence.

Surprisingly, Burdett's black mood had cleared by the time he got home and he was unusually talkative as he and Trixie ate their supper. However, at one point during the meal, he threatened to kill his wife if she ever went back to Walsford Farm. Startled, Trixie turned to look at him, to see him laughing as though the threat had been intended as a joke.

Later that evening, the two went out for a walk, by chance meeting an old acquaintance. In conversation, Frank casually asked the man if he might borrow his shotgun to do some hunting, professing himself to be bored hanging round the house and suggesting that the fresh air would do him good. Concerned that her husband might be contemplating suicide, Trixie tried to indicate that the man should refuse but, oblivious to Trixie's frantic head shaking and gesturing behind her husband's back, the man agreed to let Burdett have a gun and some ammunition.

Rather than suicide, Frank had another plan. Waiting until he knew that all the men folk at Walsford Farm would be absent, his next scheme was to visit Louise and ask her for money. Softhearted Louise could not bear the thought that her daughter might be impoverished and, ignoring her husband's instructions, handed over the sum of £18 from her life savings (more than £800 at today's value). Yet the money provided nothing more than a temporary prop and, before too long, Trixie and Frank were destitute again.

On 30 October 1930, Trixie woke in the early hours of the morning to find her husband getting dressed. When she asked him where he was going, he told her that he was unable to sleep and was going for a walk, promising to be back in half an hour. When he had not returned in forty-five minutes, a worried Trixie rang the police, telling them that her husband had gone out and that she was concerned about him.

As she put the telephone down, she noticed a stark white envelope propped up on the sideboard, the word 'WILL' written on the front. When she opened it, she found a brief note in Frank's handwriting inside: 'The time has come to end everything. I am going to do away with myself. I leave everything to my wife'.

Trixie hurriedly dressed and set off for the only place she could think of where Frank might have gone – Walsford Farm.

There, the morning chores were about to begin. Thomas had just woken Alfred, since it was his turn to milk the sixty dairy cows. As Alfred got out of bed and began to get dressed, he suddenly heard a commotion coming from his parent's bedroom – a shout from his father, a scream from his mother, then the unmistakeable sound of two gunshots. Sprinting along the landing, Alfred tried the door of his mother and father's room but there seemed to be something inside that was preventing the door from opening. Eventually, Alfred managed to open the door just enough to put his head round it and found himself staring into the double barrels of a shotgun held by a demented Frank Burdett.

'I'll do for the whole f****** lot of you!' screamed Burdett, his face contorted with rage. 'I will have you all, one at a time.'

Alfred had no reason to doubt his words. Slamming the bedroom door shut, he took off as fast as he could. Rousing his brothers as he went, he left the house and headed for a neighbour's smallholding to call the police. Meanwhile, his three brothers concealed themselves about the farm.

Archibald and Maurice chose a cow stall in which to hide, but before too long Burdett had found them. As he stood in the doorway of the barn, raising the shotgun to fire, the brothers managed to duck behind the farm's bull and, as Frank struggled to make his way round it, they scrambled out of a rear door into the fields and ran for their lives.

By this time, Alfred had reached the home of neighbour Mr Humphreys, to find that Humphreys didn't have a telephone. Mr Humphreys's son was sent into Wimborne to summon the police and, shortly afterwards, PCs Fudge and Boggust arrived at Walsford Farm, finding it seemingly deserted.

Proceeding cautiously, only too aware that a crazed gunman might still be lurking anywhere on the premises, the two officers walked through the house until they reached the master bedroom. There they found Louise, still in her nightdress, dead from a gunshot wound to her chest and shoulder. Thomas lay partly underneath the couple's bed, also dead. The presence of two spent cartridges in the bedroom indicated to the police that whoever had shot the Holloways had reloaded his gun.

Superintendent Alfred Thomas and Dr Thompson arrived at the farm just as the two police officers finished their search of the premises. With the knowledge that a deranged man was roaming the area with a loaded shotgun, the four unarmed men courageously set off to look for him.

They had gone less than 100 yards when they spotted Frank Burdett sitting on a bank at the side of a narrow country track, known locally as Muddy Lane. As the search party drew nearer, they could see that the shotgun was between his legs, barrel upwards and that the left side of Burdett's face had been completely shot away.

Amazingly, Burdett was still alive and conscious, trying desperately to speak but unable to form intelligible words. Realising that there was little that he could do to help, Dr Thompson gave him an injection of morphine for the pain and, while they waited for an ambulance to arrive, the police searched Burdett's pockets, finding four more live cartridges. Burdett had come prepared to completely eliminate the Holloway family, with a cartridge for each of the four boys.

Burdett was taken by ambulance to the Wimborne Workhouse Infirmary, where he died only hours later from a combination of blood loss and shock. The police and doctor went back to Walsford Farm to deal with the bodies of Mr and Mrs Holloway. By now, Trixie had reached the farm and met up with two of her brothers, who were aware that their parents had been shot dead, but were not aware that their killer had been found. On hearing the news of her parents' death, Trixie collapsed in a dead faint and her two brothers carried her to a neighbour's house.

As there was no doubt in anyone's mind as to who had killed Frank and Louise Holloway; there was no real police investigation, only an inquest into their deaths. There, the jury were read letters written by Frank Burdett that indicated that he was insane at the time of the shootings. The jury predictably gave their verdict that Frank Hawkeswood Burdett had committed premeditated and wilful murder and suicide, donating their fees to the Wimborne Cottage Hospital.

All that was left was to bury the dead. Burdett's funeral took place at St John's Church, Wimborne. As the Revd B. Herklots prepared to conduct the service, he was interrupted by the arrival of Mr Taylor, the clerk to the Burial Board, who informed him that, as a suicide, Burdett could not be buried in consecrated ground. Both the undertaker, Mr Elcock, and the vicar objected, the undertaker reminding Taylor that the plot had been paid for and the vicar pointing out that other suicide victims had been buried there in the recent past and stating that Burdett had the right to a Christian funeral, but Taylor was adamant – Burdett could not be buried in his freshly dug grave.

The vicar was keen to continue to argue the case, calling Taylor's decision bloody-minded but, aware of a crowd of interested spectators gathering around the outside of the cemetery, Elcock eventually backed down, instructing his men to dig a new grave in unconsecrated ground. However, this decision raised still more problems, since Herklots was now unable to conduct the burial. Watched by Burdett's only mourner, his devoted wife Trixie, Elcock lowered Burdett's coffin into the new grave, improvising a few words of the burial service as he did so.

In sharp contrast, the funeral for Frank and Louise Holloway was a massive affair and extra police had to be drafted into Wimborne to control the crowds who lined the streets on the route to Wimborne Minster where the service was held. Local businesses closed their doors as a mark of respect and the cemetery was packed to capacity.

Nothing is recorded of the subsequent fate of Trixie who, in one terrible day of appalling violence, lost her husband and both parents. It is to be hoped that she somehow found happiness in later life.

[Note: In some cotemporary accounts of the shootings, Burdett's name is alternatively spelled Frank Hawkswood Burdett. Walsford Farm is also referred to as Walford Farm.]

17

'I HAVE FELT THAT SOMEONE, SOMEWHERE, KNOWS SOMETHING'

Tarrant Keynston, 1931

On 1 October 1931, Frederick George Deamen reported for work as usual at the Coverdale Kennels in Tarrant Keynston. A local businessman, Ethelbert Frampton, had opened the kennels two years earlier and there were normally between forty and fifty dogs housed there while being trained to become gun dogs.

On that Thursday morning, kennel manager Ted Welham asked eighteen-year-old Deamen to locate Peter, a blind spaniel, who had wandered into a kale field across the road from the kennels. As Deamen searched for the dog, he heard the sound of a gunshot but, knowing that his boss often took pot shots at the pigeons or jackdaws that flew near his office, Deamen paid little attention to the noise.

Having finally located Peter, Deamen walked back to the kennels with the dog, noticing as he approached that the door to the corrugated iron hut used as Welham's office was slightly ajar, exactly as it had been when he had left it. However, when Deamen went into the office, things were far from normal. To his horror, the young kennel assistant found his boss sprawled unconscious on the floor of the hut with gunshot wounds to his head.

Deamen ran the 300 yards to the home of the Hathaway family where Welham lodged. Mary, the sixteen-year-old daughter of the house, who also worked part-time as a kennel assistant, answered his frantic knocking at the door. 'Oh, Miss Hathaway, Teddy's shot!' gasped Deamen breathlessly.

The Coverdale Training Kennels at Tarrant Keynston at the time of the shooting. (Daily Echo, Bournemouth)

Mary, her mother Edith and Deamen rushed back towards the kennels, joined on their way by Mary's father, Tom. Deamen was sent to telephone for a doctor and, just as he was leaving, Mary's two brothers, Harold and William, arrived to see what all the commotion was about.

Welham was lying on his back in his office, his shotgun on the floor beneath him. His fountain pen lay on the floor nearby and his jacket was unbuttoned, exposing his wallet, which protruded from his inside pocket. He was taken to Blandford Cottage hospital but died the following day without ever regaining consciousness.

The first police officer to arrive on the scene, PC Head, quickly reached the conclusion that Welham had committed suicide. Yet, strangely, Welham had only been appointed kennel manager after the previous manager, William Steer, had died by shooting in December 1929. Steer's body had been found in a badger sett in nearby Ashley Wood and, like his successor, a recently discharged shotgun lay close to his body with a live cartridge still in one barrel.

The inquest into Steer's death had recorded a verdict of accidental death, the shotgun having been in close contact with his clothing when the trigger was pulled. It later emerged that Steer had financial difficulties and may even have committed suicide. Yet the same could not be said about Welham, a popular man who was described as being happy and having a particularly cheery disposition. On the day prior to his death, Welham had written several business letters and their content indicated that he fully expected to deal with the replies.

Only when the inquest into Welham's death opened two days later was it pointed out that the gunshot wounds were to the back of his head and neck and also his left shoulder blade. The distribution of shotgun pellets illustrated on an X-ray seemed to show that he had been shot from behind. Dr Kenneth Wilson, who carried out the post-mortem examination, surmised that Welham had been leaning forwards when the gun was fired and stated that it was doubtful whether he would have been able to reach to pull the trigger himself.

Cottage Hospital, Blandford.

The coroner, Mr W.H. Creech, was not entirely convinced by Dr Wilson's arguments. There seemed to be no evidence to indicate the presence of any third party at the scene of the crime and the gun, which belonged to the dead man, had been found underneath his body. PC Head was still firmly convinced that Welham had committed suicide and the coroner appeared to agree with him, but eventually erred on the side of caution by adjourning the inquest to allow further enquiries to be made.

The local police force immediately called in reinforcements in the form of Detective Chief Inspector Walter Hambrook and Detective Sergeant Bell from Scotland Yard and Home Office pathologist Sir Bernard Spilsbury. Their first action was to order the postponement of Welham's funeral so that Spilsbury could conduct a second post-mortem. During this examination, Spilsbury placed the body in a sitting position on the mortuary table, with the head bent forward and was thus able to show that Welham had been shot from behind, while he was bending forwards either over or near his desk. It was possible, said Spilsbury, that Welham had realised what was happening and had ducked to try and avoid the shot. However, since he felt that the gun had been fired from a distance of several feet away, Spilsbury also stated that it would have been impossible for Welham to pull the trigger himself.

The police then called in two gunsmiths who conducted some experiments using Welham's gun. By firing the gun at a target from various distances and comparing the pattern of shot holes with those found on the walls of Welham's office, the experts reached the conclusion that the gun had been fired from the direction of the office door, at a distance of between 12ft and 15ft, most probably from around 12ft 6in.

Next, the police concentrated their efforts on trying to find out if there was any link between the deaths of Welham and the previous kennel manager, William Steer. Steer had died from gunshot wounds to the abdomen and the inquest jury had retuned a verdict of accidental death. It appeared from the way that Steer's body had been discovered that the trigger of his shot gun might have caught on a twig, causing the gun to fire accidentally. Hambrook could find no reason to doubt this scenario, thus deciding that the two deaths were unconnected and any similarities between them completely coincidental.

The investigating officers then focused their attention on events leading up to the shooting. They established that, as he often did, Welham had gone shooting with eighteen-year-old Harold Hathaway the evening before his death. Hathaway had cleaned both the twelve-bore shotgun that the men had taken with them and Welham's sixteen-bore gun, which was usually kept in a cupboard near his desk. On returning from their evening's shooting, Hathaway had replaced the twelve-bore gun in the cupboard next to Welham's gun. Welham had behaved normally all evening and had been in good spirits.

On the morning of the shooting, Welham had arrived for work as usual at around 7.15 a.m. At 8 a.m., he had returned to his lodgings for breakfast, going back to the kennels an hour later, when he then sent his assistant off to look for the blind spaniel. The shot had been heard by Deamen and other villagers at about 9.30 a.m. and, at 9.40 a.m., Deaman had arrived at the Hathaway's cottage with the news of the tragedy.

Members of the local community were interviewed and the police soon realised that, while most people firmly believed that Welham had committed suicide, tongues were wagging and a number of rumours about his death were circulating. The first of these was that Welham – and indeed Steer – had been murdered by someone with a personal grudge against the kennels. Then there was gossip about Welham's love life. The thirty-one-year-old kennel manager had broken off an engagement some time previously and was now supposedly keeping company with a young woman who lived near to the kennels. He had also allegedly been seen with another woman who lived at nearby Wimborne. Had he been murdered by a jealous love rival or even a spurned woman?

This latter theory was somewhat strengthened by the reported sighting of an attractive young woman, dressed in a white hooded coat, near the kennels at around the time of the shooting. Nobody could provide any logical explanation why a woman should have been walking alone on the isolated country lane so early in the morning.

Could robbery have been a motive for someone to shoot Welham? He had 10s in his wallet when his body was found and there were nine pounds locked in a drawer in the office. However, his employer, Frampton, believed that Welham should have had at least £10 on his person. A horse rider came forward to say that, on the morning of the murder, while riding near the kennels, he had been approached by a middle-aged man who, after asking the time, had become aggressive and demanded to be given some money. Later in the day, an attempt was made to snatch money from the till of a public house at nearby Wimborne. The would-be raider, again described as a middle-aged man, had fled empty handed after being confronted by the pub landlady.

The inquest into Welham's death was reconvened and adjourned on 10 and 23 October, yet the police seemed no nearer to finding the identity of his killer. Whoever had committed the murder had managed to choose a window of approximately ten minutes while Deamen was out searching for the missing spaniel, leaving the victim alone in his office. The killer had somehow managed to avoid disturbing the forty or so dogs on the premises since no unusual barking had been heard. He – or she – had removed the victim's shotgun from its place in the cupboard near the desk and loaded it, apparently without Welham noticing. Then, having fired the gun, the killer staged a suicide by placing the weapon under Welham's body.

Welham was known to be extremely careful with firearms and it was unthinkable that he would have kept a loaded gun in his office unless he was intending to use it. Harold Hathaway had cleaned the gun only hours before the murder and replaced it unloaded in the cupboard. Welham had no known enemies and did not appear to be in the frame of mind to commit suicide.

Eventually, on 27 October and with no new evidence, the coroner's jury returned a verdict of 'wilful murder by person or persons unknown' and the coroner formally closed the inquest, making a final appeal to the public via the press. 'I have felt that someone, somewhere – I don't say among the witnesses – knows something but has said nothing. If there be any such person, be it witness or one who has never given any opinion, they are standing in a very precarious position if they do not make known what they know'.

With no further leads to follow, the officers returned to Scotland Yard and life carried on as normal in the hamlet of Tarrant Keynston. It was an especially busy time for young Fred Deamen. On 30 October, he appeared before magistrates at Wimborne, charged with the theft of a camera from Ethelbert Frampton and a pair of gloves from the Coverdale Kennels.

Deamen denied both charges, maintaining that he had bought the camera from a man he had met on his way home from work and that the gloves had been discarded by their owner and left lying around at the kennels dirty and covered in mildew. He had taken them in the belief that they were no longer wanted. In the event, both charges against him were dismissed but, just a day or two later, Deamen had an accident while riding his motorcycle and was rushed to hospital semi-conscious.

It was while Deamen was recovering from his injuries in hospital that the investigations into the murder of his boss took an unexpected turn, bringing police rushing back to Dorset from Scotland Yard.

After first consulting with Ethelbert Frampton, Tom Hathaway approached the local police saying that he wished to amend his statement made after the discovery of the body. In an interview with Chief Inspector Hambrook, Hathaway now revealed that, on entering Welham's office, he had noticed a hazel stick and a piece of string lying near the body. Thinking to spare Welham's family the ordeal of discovering that he had committed suicide, he had surreptitiously slipped the 2ft 9in length of string into his pocket and removed the hazel stick to which it was attached to a corner of the office.

Hathaway had assumed that a verdict of accidental death would be returned at the inquest. Now, with a verdict of murder, he was afraid that someone might be arrested for a crime that hadn't actually been committed. Although he undoubtedly meant well, Hathaway's actions had muddied the waters of the investigation and may have allowed Welham's killer to walk free.

Hathaway's revelations prompted a new round of experiments with Welham's gun, this time making use of the piece of string found at the scene, which Hathaway had kept and handed over to the police. However, rather than proving that Welham had committed suicide, the string finally and conclusively confirmed that his death had been murder, since it was far too short to have been used to fire the weapon given the distance from which it had been discharged. Even PC Head, who until this point had been unshakeable in his belief that Welham had committed suicide, was forced to concede that he had been wrong. All that the string and hazel stick showed was that the killer had been even more inventive in his or her attempts to make the killing look like suicide, indicating that the murder had been premeditated rather than the result of a sudden impulse in the heat of passion.

The murder of Edward Welham remains unsolved to this day.

18

'I DID IT DELIBERATELY AND I'D DO IT AGAIN'

Bournemouth, 1935

'Do you know that you have a lovely face?' asked the young woman. The recipient of this compliment was astounded.

'Great Scott! Have I?' he exclaimed. 'I'm going home right now to have a look at it. I never thought it worth looking at yet.'

'I'm not joking', insisted the woman. 'You have almost the kindest face I ever saw.'

Little did either the man or the woman know that these flattering words would eventually lead to a marriage, extra-marital affairs, scandal and, ultimately, murder.

The young woman was Alma Victoria Pakenham, a Canadian concert pianist; the man was Francis Mawson Rattenbury, an elderly British architect working in Canada. The couple first met in 1922 after a piano recital given by Alma at a hotel in British Columbia. Relaxing in the hotel lounge with a friend after her performance, Alma heard the rousing strains of 'For He's a Jolly Good Fellow' coming from another part of the hotel and casually remarked that the singers seemed really sincere in their sentiments. Curiosity drew her to investigate the celebrations more closely and she soon discovered that the object of the adulation was Rattenbury, famed for his innovative design of the Canadian parliament buildings, the Law Courts in Vancouver and the Empress Hotel in Victoria. Alma was impressed by his good looks and self-confidence and, when the two were eventually introduced, Rattenbury found himself equally smitten by the vivacious and mercurial Alma.

Empress Hotel, Victoria, B. C.

The Empress Hotel, 1909.

Although then only twenty-nine years old, Alma had already led a full and interesting life. Aged nineteen, she had married for the first time to a man from Ulster, with whom she had moved to England. Tragically, he had died during the First World War in the Battle of the Somme and, as soon as Alma heard of his death, she joined a Scottish ambulance unit, working behind enemy lines in France. Such was her bravery that she was awarded the Croix de Guerre Medal, with Star and Palm.

When the war ended, she married again, this time to a captain, and the couple moved to America. The marriage broke up after the birth of a son, Christopher, and Alma and her child moved back to Canada to live with her aunt in Victoria.

Now, it seemed, she had another suitor. Having made a point of attending one of her piano recitals, Rattenbury met Alma again by chance shortly afterwards at a dance and, by the end of the evening the couple had fallen in love.

They met at a time when things were not going well for Francis Rattenbury. The fifty-five-year-old man was feeling his age. He had lost interest in his work, complained of several physical afflictions, and was, to the concern of his friends, beginning to look old and unwell. He and his wife of more than twenty years were drifting apart and he was depressed and lethargic. Attracting the attentions of Alma, a woman thirty years his junior, must have acted as a real tonic.

By 1925, Rattenbury's wife had left him, citing her husband's affair with Alma as grounds for divorce. Alma, too, had arranged a divorce from her estranged husband and she and Rattenbury married and moved into his house at Oak Bay with Christopher, who was then three years old. However, their May to December marriage was not well received in Canadian society and eventually Francis moved his wife and stepson back to England where they could make a fresh start.

Manor Road, Bournemouth, 1906.

The family settled into the Villa Madeira on Manor Road, Bournemouth, from where Anna embraced a new career as a songwriter, writing under the pseudonym 'Lozanne'. She was quite successful in her new venture and several of her compositions were recorded and played on BBC radio.

In due course, Alma gave birth to the couple's son, John, and subsequently fell ill with tuberculosis. In the meantime, Francis once again began to feel his advancing years. Alma was quite extravagant and, having now retired, Francis worried about money. He was also finding it somewhat of a strain being married to a much younger woman. He and Alma had not shared a bed since John's birth six years previously, and it was almost certain that the still young and highly sexed Alma had taken lovers to compensate for her husband's deficiencies in the bedroom.

By 1935, Rattenbury had fallen into another of his frequent bouts of depression and, on Sunday 24 March, Alma found herself struggling to think of ways to lift his near-suicidal mood. It was a lovely day and Bournemouth was bathed in warm spring sunshine, so she impulsively decided to erect an awning in the garden so that he could sit outside. However, she was unable to find a mallet with which to hammer the pegs into the ground. Stoner, the couple's chauffeur/handyman, mentioned that his grandparents owned one and Alma sent him off to borrow it. While waiting for his return, as a diversion for Francis, she arranged a trip to a nearby kennels to see a litter of puppies that her dog had just borne, but any elevation in her husband's state of mind was all too brief and by tea time that afternoon, he was back to being morose and feeling hopelessly depressed. Over tea, he insisted on reading aloud passages from a book, *Stay of Execution* by Eliot Crawshay-Williams.

Alma and Francis Rattenbury with their son, John. (Daily Echo, Bournemouth)

The main character from the novel, Stephen Clarke, was in many ways similar to Francis Rattenbury, a bitter man who feels old, depressed and suicidal. In one chapter of the book, Clarke tries to dissuade a young girl from marrying him, telling her that it would be hell for both of them. The girl would have to watch her husband 'mouldering' while she still felt 'frisky'. A woman, Clarke theorised, always wanted a good deal more sex than a man. It would take a young man all his time to keep pace with her and an old man wouldn't stand a chance of doing so, forcing the woman to seek satisfaction elsewhere.

It was at that passage that Rattenbury, whose own life mirrored the book in so many ways, finished reading. Leaving the book open at that page, he placed it face down on the piano in the drawing room. Only hours later, he was found sitting in his armchair, one eye blackened and a large pool of blood on the floor beside him.

On discovering her injured husband slumped unconscious, Alma immediately began to administer what first aid she could. Having tried to rub his cold hands, she searched for a pulse and shook him to try and bring him round. Noticing the blood on the floor, she stepped back in alarm, treading on her husband's false teeth with her bare feet as she did.

This was enough to send her into hysterics. She screamed for Irene Riggs, her housekeeper, telling her, 'Someone has hurt Ratz! Telephone the doctor.' While Irene was calling for assistance, Alma ran to the bathroom to fetch a towel, which she wrapped around Francis's head. Then she poured herself a neat whisky, gulped it down and immediately vomited it back up again.

Her telephone call finished, Irene came to help tend to her employer, fetching a bowl of water and a cloth to bathe his injured eye. Between them, the two women struggled to lift Rattenbury, eventually calling for Stoner, who helped the two women get Rattenbury to his bed. Having sent Stoner to drive to the doctor's house and hurry him up, Alma and Irene tried to undress Rattenbury. Mindful of having a small child in the house, who might become distressed by the evening's events, Anna also tried to clean up the blood in the drawing room and threw away her husband's bloody collar.

Dr O'Donnell arrived at 11.15 p.m. and asked Alma what had happened. By now Alma was well on the way to being drunk and could only tell the doctor that 'Somebody's finished him'. After a brief examination of the wound, Dr O'Donnell telephoned for Mr Rooke, a surgeon who lived locally. Rooke arrived by taxi some forty-five minutes later, but found any examination of the injured man almost impossible, since the drunk and highly excited Alma kept getting in the way. Accordingly, he arranged for Rattenbury to be moved to Strathallen Nursing Home where the two doctors were finally able to conduct a proper examination. Finding three large wounds on Rattenbury's head, they notified the police.

The first officer to arrive at the Villa Madeira was PC Arthur Bagwell, who was greeted by Alma and ushered into the drawing room. Alma's behaviour as the policeman tried in vain to interview her was bizarre to say the least. As Irene tried unsuccessfully to calm her down, she chattered incessantly, seemingly without pausing for breath, laughed hysterically and inappropriately, played records of her own songs at full volume, danced around the room and even tried to kiss the police constable.

Bagwell was forced to seek backup for his own protection and Alma tried to follow him when he left to summon reinforcements. He returned soon afterwards with a number of officers, who promptly began a search of the house.

They found the discarded collar and Rattenbury's waistcoat and jacket in the bathroom, both newly washed. The cover from the chair on which he had been sitting was in the bath.

Bagwell tried again to interview Alma and, at one point, she suddenly declared, 'I know who done it'. Bagwell cautioned her and opened his notebook in readiness but Alma continued to ramble. 'I did it with a mallet', she said. 'Ratz has lived too long. It is hidden'. She immediately contradicted herself, saying, 'No, my lover did it'. She told Constable Bagwell that the chair was covered in urine and then offered him £10.

Inspector Mills, meanwhile, had gone to the nursing home, where he had seen Stoner sitting outside in the Rattenbury's car, apparently asleep. On returning to Villa Madeira, Mills informed Alma that her husband was judged to be in a critical condition and, at this, Alma's first words were, 'Will this be against me?'

She was cautioned again but continued to ramble, telling the investigators 'I did it. He gave me the book. He has lived too long.' She asked if the coroner had yet been informed and promised to show the police the location of the mallet she had used the previous morning. She also promised to 'make a better job of it next time', stating that she had made a 'proper muddle of it' and that she 'thought she was strong enough'.

By 4 a.m., Dr O'Donnell was summoned back to the house with the purpose of administering a sedative to Alma, who was rapidly becoming more and more unhinged as the night progressed. Dr O'Donnell put her to bed and gave her half a grain of morphine to try and quieten her down, but shortly afterwards she came downstairs again and excitedly announced to the police that Rattenbury's son had committed the murder.

Aware that Rattenbury's son from his first marriage was presently in Canada, O'Donnell quietly reminded the officers that Alma had consumed a great deal of whisky and also been given morphine. As a consequence, he doubted her fitness to be questioned. Alma was, with difficulty, persuaded to go upstairs and get back into bed. After sleeping fitfully for a couple of hours, she was given a cup of coffee but was immediately sick.

By 8.15 a.m., the police had decided that Alma was fit to provide a statement. Now, she told officers that she had been playing cards with her husband when he had told her that he wanted to die and begged her to kill him. She had picked up the mallet, at which Francis Rattenbury allegedly told her that she didn't 'have the guts to do it'. At that, she hit him hard on the head, subsequently concealing the mallet outside in the garden.

She was taken to Bournemouth police station for further questioning. As she left the house, she told Irene and Stoner, 'Don't make fools of yourselves', to which Stoner responded, 'You have got yourself into this mess by talking too much.'

By now, officers had discovered a mallet bearing traces of blood and hair behind a trellis in the garden of the Villa Madeira and, at 8.45 a.m., Alma was charged with wounding or causing grievous bodily harm to her husband with intent to murder him. 'That's right', said Alma in response. 'I did it deliberately and I'd do it again'. Less than three hours later she made a brief appearance at Bournemouth Magistrates Court. She appeared dazed and confused as, on the advice of her solicitor, Mr Lewis Manning, she pleaded 'Not Guilty' to the charges against her. Having been remanded in custody, she was allowed a twenty-minute visit from Dr O'Donnell before being transported to the Royal Holloway Prison. At that visit, Dr O'Donnell noted that her pupils were still contracted as a side effect of the morphine he had administered earlier that morning and that she retched repeatedly. He also observed that Alma was unsteady on her feet and unable to stand without support.

The following day, with Alma incarcerated and Rattenbury hospitalised, the staff at the Villa Madeira found themselves at a loose end. George Stoner and Irene Riggs decided to take a day off and drive to Wimborne Minster. Stoner was in a talkative mood and, as he drove through Ensbury Park, he pointed out the homes of his family and other acquaintances to Irene. Passing his grandparents' home, he casually remarked that that was where he had collected the mallet on Sunday evening, adding that since he had worn gloves, it would not have any fingerprints on it.

Irene Riggs had been enjoying a day off on 24 March, and had been completely unaware that Stoner had borrowed a mallet or for what purpose he had been asked to obtain one. Now, she could hardly believe her ears. She thought quickly and bravely asked Stoner, 'Why did you do it?'

'I saw him making love to Alma in the afternoon', was Stoner's reply.

Irene's mind was in turmoil, believing as she now did that her mistress had confessed to a crime that she didn't commit. A few days later, on Wednesday 27 March, Irene's mother and brother moved into the Villa Madeira to keep her company and, probably after having voiced her concerns to her family, that evening Irene went to visit a priest. On her return to the house at 10.30 p.m., she discovered that Stoner, a non-drinker, had got drunk and run out of the house shouting that he had put Mrs Rattenbury in jail. He was brought home again by two local taxi drivers, but was in such a wild state that Irene was in fear for her life.

The following morning, Rattenbury lost his fight for life and Stoner caught an early train to London after receiving a letter from Alma asking him to come and visit her. Meanwhile, Dr O'Donnell called at the Villa Madeira and had a long conversation with Irene Riggs, whom he sensed was holding something back. O'Donnell eventually asked her directly if she believed that Alma had killed her husband and received the emphatic answer, 'I know that she did not!'

It appears that much of Irene's reticence to speak out was due to her unwillingness to reveal that Alma Rattenbury and George Percy Stoner had been lovers for some time. In September 1934, Stoner had responded to an advertisement in the *Bournemouth Daily Echo*, placed by the Rattenburys who wished to engage another servant. The advertisement read:

> Daily willing lad, 14–18, for housework. Scout-trained preferred. Apply between 11–12, 8–9 at 5 Manor Road, Bournemouth.

The Square, Bournemouth, 1933.

Although he was just eighteen years old at the time, on applying for the position Stoner gave his age as twenty-two and, since he was able to drive a car, was offered a position as a chauffeur/handyman.

Stoner was the only child of a working-class couple from Redhill, Bournemouth, and was a pleasant and personable young man, if rather shy. As a child, he had missed a lot of schooling and was thought of as backward. He was, however, quite handsome and also undoubtedly much more virile than the ageing, now impotent, Francis Rattenbury and, within a short time, was providing much more than his driving skills for his employers, particularly Alma, who soon became his mistress in every sense of the word.

She arranged for him to move into a spare room at the Villa Madeira and every night he would creep quietly into her bedroom. Francis Rattenbury, who slept separately from his wife, was either unaware or unconcerned by their affair, having long ago given his wife permission to make discreet arrangements to accommodate her sexual needs outside the marriage.

Had the liaison remained purely a physical one then Rattenbury might still have been alive. However, Alma fell deeply in love with the young servant and, sensing the power he had over her, the immature Stoner began to exploit her. He demanded that she stopped drinking cocktails in the evening and Alma meekly did as she was asked. At some stage in their relationship, Alma discovered her lover's true age and immediately tried to break off their affair. Stoner refused to accept the break-up and took to carrying a knife with a four-inch blade, with which he threatened to kill her. On another occasion, he lost his temper and grabbed Alma so violently that Irene Riggs was forced to step in and separate them.

In February 1935, Alma summoned Dr O'Donnell to the house. Confessing the affair to him, she told him of Stoner's violence towards her and asked for the doctor's help in respect of the drugs that Stoner was abusing. The doctor spoke with the young man, who admitted that he was taking cocaine but refused any intervention by the doctor to break him of the habit.

In the week prior to Francis Rattenbury's murder, Alma cajoled some money from her husband and, on the pretext of going to London for an operation, went off for a few days with her young lover. The couple stayed at the Royal Palace Hotel in Kensington, registering as brother and sister. For three days they attended cinemas and theatres and went shopping at Harrods, where Alma treated Stoner to a new wardrobe of clothes, including silk pyjamas.

When they returned to the Villa Madeira on 22 March, it was to find Francis Rattenbury in the depths of depression. Alma suggested a trip to London to try and raise his spirits, but her husband showed no interest in such an excursion. However, he did show some enthusiasm for visiting a friend in Bridport, with whom he wanted to discuss a business project.

Relieved to have found something to lighten her husband's dark mood, Alma went into his bedroom to telephone the friend and make arrangements for a visit. Mr Jenks invited the Rattenburys to stay overnight – something to which Stoner had violent objections.

During her telephone conversation with Mr Jenks, Stoner burst into the room waving a toy pistol, which Alma believed at the time was a real gun. Stoner was furious to find

Alma in her husband's bedroom with the door closed, immediately jumping to the conclusion that the couple had been engaged in some sexual activity.

He angrily forbade Alma to go into her husband's bedroom and close the door again, and insisted that, if the Rattenburys went to Bridport the next day, he was not going to drive them. Having reassured Stoner that she and her husband would be sleeping in separate rooms in Bridport, Stoner left the room and Alma assumed that the argument between them was over and went about her evening routine as normal.

She packed some clothes for the proposed trip to Bridport the following day, gave young John a bath and tucked him into bed. She then joined her husband in the drawing room and the couple played cards until about 9.30 p.m. when, after kissing Francis goodnight, she let out her dog, Dinah, then went to bed.

Before finally retiring for the night, Alma slipped into Irene Riggs' bedroom for a ten-minute chat about arrangements for the following day before returning to her own room, where she was shortly joined by Stoner. Noticing that Stoner seemed agitated, Alma asked him what the matter was. Stoner confessed that he was in trouble, but refused to tell her in what way. Alma pressed him for an answer and continued to do so until he reluctantly told her that she would not be going to Bridport in the morning because he had hurt 'Ratz'.

At this point, Alma heard a groan from downstairs and rushed down to discover her husband sitting in his chair, bleeding profusely from wounds to his head.

Once Irene Riggs was assured that Dr O'Donnell knew all about Alma's illicit affair with Stoner, she reluctantly told the doctor that Stoner had confessed to her that he, not Alma, had been the one to murder Francis Rattenbury. Armed with this knowledge, Dr O'Donnell felt he had no choice but to inform the police, and Stoner was arrested at Bournemouth station as he returned from what had proved to be a wasted attempt to visit his mistress in prison. When apprehended he was carrying a letter from Alma, two photographs of her and a gold watch that she given him, which he told the arresting officers was worth £20.

Detained at the police station overnight, the following morning he asked to talk with an officer. He opened the conversation with a question, asking the officer, 'You know Mrs Rattenbury, don't you?' When the policeman confirmed that he did, Stoner continued 'Do you know that she had nothing to do with this affair?' Stoner was immediately cautioned but nevertheless went on to confess that it was he who had killed Francis Rattenbury. He had been watching from the garden through the French windows and had seen Alma kissing her husband goodnight. Consumed with jealousy, he had crept in through the unlocked windows and hit Rattenbury three times over the head with a mallet. The elderly gentleman had been dozing in his chair and had no time to defend himself, said Stoner.

He ended his confession by suggesting that a doctor was present when the news of his arrest was broken to Alma Rattenbury, predicting that she would 'go out of her mind'.

Stoner and Alma next met when they appeared together at Dorchester Assizes, the charges against Alma having been elevated to murder after the death of her husband. The hearing lasted for three days before both defendants were committed for trial at the Old Bailey.

Confined in Holloway Prison, awaiting the start of her trial, Alma continued to try and protect Stoner, insisting that she alone was responsible for the murder of her husband. Her lawyers continually tried to persuade her to tell the truth, as did Dr Morton, the then governor of Holloway, who was convinced that she was innocent. In the end, it took a visit from Alma's young son, Christopher, to change her mind.

Christopher was being cared for by his aunt, Daphne Kingham, the sister of Alma's second husband, Compton Pakenham. Mrs Kingham visited Alma regularly in prison and, having previously failed to get Alma to admit the truth about Rattenbury's murder, decided to pile on the pressure by taking the boy with her on one of her visits.

Alma was a conscientious mother, who adored her children and, after Mrs Kingham pointed out that the boys would be forever afterwards known as the sons of a woman hanged for murder, she began to have second thoughts about shielding her lover. In a letter to Irene Riggs, she wrote of her love for her boys and hinted for the first time that she might be having a change of heart. By the time the trial opened at The Old Bailey on 27 May, it appeared she had finally made up her mind. Both defendants entered pleas of 'Not Guilty', at which point Alma's counsel, Terence O'Connor, leaned across and whispered to J.D. Casswell, who was acting for Stoner, 'Mrs Rattenbury is going to give evidence against your boy.'

This information came as a complete surprise to Casswell. He was aware that Stoner was still insisting that he alone was responsible for Rattnbury's murder and that he was more interested in ensuring that Alma was not convicted than he was in establishing his own innocence. Now, with the news that Alma was going to testify against his client, Casswell began to realise the hopelessness of his task. He had been instructed to say in Stoner's defence that the young man had been under the influence of cocaine at the time of the murder and therefore could not be held responsible for his actions. (This was in spite of the fact that Stoner was unable even to describe the appearance of cocaine when questioned about his use of the drug, insisting that it was brown with black flecks.)

Casswell approached the trial judge, Mr Justice Humphreys, with an application for the two defendants to be tried separately. In separate trials, Alma's letter to Irene Riggs, in which she intimated that she was intending to abandon Stoner and save herself, could not be admitted into evidence. The judge dismissed the motion for separate trials, stating that he would deal with the admissibility of the letter when the need arose.

Although Stoner and Alma Rattenbury had not been charged with conspiracy to murder, which would have involved proving some collusion between them in the plan to kill Rattenbury, the prosecuting counsel, Mr R.C. Croom-Johnson KC, opened the proceedings with an eighty-minute speech designed to demonstrate to the jury that both had been equally responsible. His most important witness was Irene Riggs, who related the events on the night of the murder and told of Stoner's confession to her of his guilt on the subsequent trip to Wimborne Minster.

In the case against Alma, the statements that she made to the police in the hours immediately following the attack on her husband, which included her confessions, were crucial to the prosecution. However, whereas the police insisted that Alma had been perfectly fit to give a statement the morning afterwards, Dr O'Donnell strongly disagreed.

He testified to the fact that Alma was very drunk and under the influence of morphine and that he would give little credence to any statement that she had given that morning. Dr O'Donnell's testimony was supported by prison governor Mr Morton, who told the court that Alma had still been confused on her admission to prison.

Finally, Alma herself took the stand. Described as a pretty woman, looking much younger than her thirty-eight years, she was smartly dressed in a dark blue coat with matching hat and gloves. Initially, her evidence was given so quietly that she had to be urged by her counsel to speak up. From then on, she gave her evidence in a firm, clear voice, appearing composed at all times.

Having described her relationship with her husband and finding him dreadfully injured, she went on to state that she had absolutely no memory of the police attending immediately after the attack. Casswell, defending Stoner, found himself hampered by his inability to cross-examine Alma Rattenbury, so keen was his client to protect his mistress. Meanwhile, Stoner listened to the proceedings without emotion, only becoming slightly more animated when Alma Rattenbury recounted details of their passionate affair. When she acknowledged to the court, 'I love him', his eyes briefly filled with tears.

Stoner was not called to give evidence since Casswell maintained that, as he was allegedly under the influence of cocaine at the time of the attack on Francis Rattenbury, his recollections of the offence would not be accurate.

The jury retired on the fifth day of the trial, returning about three-quarters of an hour later with their verdicts. Alma Victoria Rattenbury was found not guilty of the murder of Francis Rattenbury. George Percy Stoner was pronounced guilty.

As the verdict was announced, Alma took a step forward and reached out towards Stoner. She was heard to say, 'Oh, no. Oh, no', then was escorted from the dock by prison wardresses to hear the judge pronounce sentence of death on Stoner. Asked by the judge if he had anything to say as to why the death sentence should not be passed upon him, Stoner replied, 'Nothing at all, sir' – the only words he had spoken throughout the entire proceedings. As he was led from the court, Alma Rattenbury was brought back to the dock to face a second charge of being an accessory after the act of murder. Her composure now completely gone, she hung limp and weeping between the two wardresses, her pale face smudged with tears as the prosecution offered no evidence against her and the charge was dismissed. Moments later, as she was leaving the court, she came face to face with Stoner. She tried to speak but was so choked with emotion that she was unable to do so. Stoner merely smiled at her. He was later to tell his father that he was perfectly content. They had set Alma free and that was all that mattered to him.

Alma was taken to the home of her late husband's nephew but the house was besieged, both by reporters and by a hostile crowd who sympathised with Stoner, casting Alma as a wicked woman who had led an innocent boy astray. Eventually, she moved to a nursing home in Bayswater.

While there, she gave instructions that no expense was to be spared in helping Stoner and made repeated unsuccessful efforts to gain permission to visit him in prison. She also announced her intention to commit suicide at the very moment that Stoner was executed.

On 2 June, she left the nursing home and moved to another one in Devonshire Street. The following day, she quietly slipped away, catching a train for Bournemouth at Waterloo station. She eventually left the train at Christchurch, near to the location of Christopher's boarding school, but rather than visiting him, found herself walking through the meadows towards Three Arches Bend on the River Avon.

Sitting on the grass in the sunshine, she took a couple of old envelopes and a pencil from her handbag, lit a cigarette and began to write a note. She described how she had already tried to jump under a train, then a bus, but had been thwarted by the fact that there were too many people about. She asked God to bless her children and look after them, then ended the note, 'Thank God for peace at last'.

A little while later, a farm worker spotted a woman walking determinedly towards the riverbank. As he watched, the woman dropped into a squatting position and slowly toppled forwards head first into the water. Thinking that she had simply overbalanced while picking flowers, he rushed to her assistance, finding her floating face upwards about five yards from the bank. A non-swimmer, the man tried in vain to reach the woman, first with his foot, then by throwing her coat, which she had left on the bank. All the while, the woman watched him, her face blank, seemingly oblivious to his efforts to rescue her.

As the farm worker watched in horror, the woman drifted out towards the centre of the river. Only then did he notice the blood oozing from her chest and tainting the water. Alma had stabbed herself six times in the chest, puncturing her left lung in four places and wounding her heart.

Informed of her death, Stoner broke down and sobbed. Now he wrote to his defence counsel professing his innocence and stating that Alma's death had freed him to give a true account of the murder. An appeal was held on 24 June, at which Casswell again argued that the two defendants should have been tried separately, and he complained that the trial judge had skipped over the evidence that Stoner was under the influence of cocaine at the time of the murder. Stoner, said Casswell, had not given evidence for fear of incriminating the woman he loved. Now that woman was dead, and Stoner should be given a fresh opportunity to state his case. However, the appeal judge, Lord Chief Justice Hewart, would have none of Casswell's protestations, dismissing the appeal as 'a waste of time'.

Yet, the following day, Home Secretary Sir John Simon announced that he was commuting Stoner's sentence to one of penal servitude for life. He had received a petition with 320,000 signatures appealing for clemency for the young man but had not wanted to make a decision while the appeal was pending.

In the event, Stoner served just seven years of his sentence, being released from prison in 1942, aged twenty-six, having been a model prisoner. He immediately joined the Army and went on to take part in the D-Day landings. He returned from the war to live at Redhill, where he married and became a responsible member of the community until his death in Christchurch Hospital in 2000, aged eighty-three. Coincidentally, his death occurred on the 65th anniversary of the murder of Francis Rattenbury, only about half a mile from the spot on the River Avon where his beloved Alma had perished.

Francis Rattenbury's grave, 2008. (© N. Sly)

Alma's two boys both grew up to be successful professional men, John following in his father's footsteps to become an architect, working in America. In a recent interview with *The Times* newspaper, given on the occasion of a revival of a play, *Cause Celebre*, written about the trial by Terence Rattigan, John mentions that he bears no ill will towards Stoner. Rather, he views him as a victim of circumstance, an impressionable young man who suddenly found himself the object of the affections of a beautiful older woman and was too immature to cope.

It has since been suggested that the true motive for Francis Rattenbury's murder was that Stoner overheard a suggestion made by him that Alma should have an affair with Mr Jenks in Bridport in order to encourage him to finance Rattenbury's proposed business project. According to Alma's former sister-in-law, Mrs Kingham, Stoner became so enraged at the thought of his mistress being prostituted by her husband for his financial gain that he was driven to murder him. As all of the participants in this tragedy are now deceased, it is unlikely that the full truth of the matter will ever come to light.

19

'I'VE BEEN A GOOD WIFE TO HIM AND NOBODY CAN SAY I HAVEN'T'

Coombe, 1935

Nineteen-year-old Charlotte McHugh, an illiterate Irish gypsy girl, once believed that she had found her prince charming in the form of an English soldier. Frederick John Bryant was a military policeman serving with the Dorset regiment and met Charlotte when he was sent to Londonderry, one of 60,000 English soldiers dispatched to assist in the repression of the Sinn Fein movement during the Irish troubles of 1917–22.

When Bryant left Ireland to return to civilian life and his job as a cowman in Dorset, Charlotte went with him. The couple married in March 1922 at Wells in Somerset, and settled in a tied cottage at Nether Compton, near Sherborne.

However, life in rural Dorset wasn't the idyll of Charlotte's dreams. She had simply exchanged poverty and squalor in Ireland for the same in England. Frequently, she sought relief from her desperate circumstances by visiting the local pub, where she became known amongst the locals as 'Compton Liz', 'Black Bess' or 'Killarney Kate'. As well as gaining several nicknames, Charlotte also gained a reputation for accepting drinks from strange men, many of whom were subsequently invited back to the cottage she shared with Frederick.

Not only were these liaisons extremely pleasurable for Charlotte, but they were also a means of supplementing the meagre 38*s* her husband received as his weekly wage.

Charlotte Bryant. (Daily Echo, Bournemouth)

Bryant was well aware of his wife's extra-marital activities and even condoned them. 'I don't care what she does', he told a neighbour who had informed him of Charlotte's visitors. 'Four pounds a week is better than thirty bob.'

Charlotte had pretensions to an extravagant lifestyle. On occasions, she was known to buy luxury foodstuffs and she also sometimes hired a car and driver for a day, the cost of which was almost the equivalent of a week's wage for her husband. To support her aspirations, Charlotte became adept at thinking of new ways to extract money from her gentleman callers. On one occasion, she managed to convince a Yeovil businessman that she was carrying his baby. The man – doubtless terrified of the likely scandal – quickly handed over £25 to pay for an abortion but, months later, Charlotte returned with a baby in her arms, demanding regular child support payments. In fact, the baby was fathered by neither the businessman nor Charlotte's husband, but was the progeny of one of her most regular lovers, Leonard Parsons.

Parsons – or Bill Moss as he was sometimes known – was a travelling salesman and horse dealer with a gypsy background and nomadic lifestyle similar to Charlotte's own. Moss lived with Priscilla Loveridge on Huish gypsy camp at Weston-super-Mare. Together they had four illegitimate children. However, once he met Charlotte and became her lover in 1933, Parsons all but moved in with the Bryant family. Surprisingly under the circumstances, he and Frederick Bryant became good friends, often drinking together at the Crown public house and even sharing a razor.

It was while Parsons was staying at the cottage that Fred Bryant suffered the first episode of what was to become a prolonged illness. On 13 May Bryant went to work as usual, while Parsons left to conduct some business, taking with him Charlotte and Ernest, the Bryant's oldest child. Fred ate the lunch of meat, potatoes and peas left for him by Charlotte and, shortly afterwards, became seriously ill with what looked like food poisoning.

Weakened by severe vomiting and diarrhoea, all Fred could do was to call out for his next-door neighbour, Mrs Ethel Staunton. When Mrs Staunton heard his cries, she immediately went to see if she could help, finding Fred sitting on the stairs, groaning and shivering violently. Fred asked her to fetch a tin bath from the garden, which she did, making him a solution of salt water to induce vomiting. She then went off to fetch her husband, Bernard.

By the time she came back, Frederick Bryant had managed to drag himself upstairs to bed. He had also vomited into the bath, bringing up a large quantity of what Mr Staunton described as 'green frothy stuff'. Staunton sent someone to telephone for the doctor and, while waiting for him to arrive, made up several hot water bottles for his neighbour who was complaining of feeling bitterly cold.

Dr McCarthy eventually arrived to find Frederick Bryant complaining of stomach pains and cramp in his legs and suffering from bouts of severe sickness and diarrhoea. Concluding that his patient had an attack of food poisoning, he gave him an injection and left him to rest. When he called back at the cottage the next day, he found Bryant's condition to have greatly improved. Charlotte Bryant was attending to him and McCarthy questioned her about what her husband had eaten over the previous couple of days. Charlotte assured him that Fred had eaten exactly the same food as the rest of the family and that nobody else had suffered any ill effects, which appeared to rule out food poisoning as the cause of Fred's illness.

Fred eventually made a full recovery but, on 6 August, he again fell ill with similar symptoms. This time he was diagnosed with gastroenteritis and, once more, after a few days, he was back to his normal rude health.

In October 1935, the Bryant family moved to a new cottage at Coombe. It was around this time that Leonard Parsons' attraction for Charlotte began to show signs of waning. Afraid that he was about to leave her, Charlotte tried numerous ways to keep him by her side. First, she hid his clothes. A few days later, she visited a garage where he had left his car for repairs. Posing as Mrs Parsons, she told the garage owner to be careful about working on the car since her husband had no means of paying the bill.

Her efforts were in vain as, in November, Parsons left the Bryant household never to return. Charlotte, however, had no intention of letting him get away and made strenuous effort to track him down. She hired a car and driver to take her to the Huish Camp to see Priscilla Loveridge. Priscilla wasn't there on that day, but Charlotte managed to speak to her mother, Mrs Penfold, telling her that she wanted to open her daughter's eyes to the baby her partner had fathered. Mrs Penfold asked Charlotte if she had a husband, to which Charlotte replied that she had, but that he was seriously ill in a nursing home and she didn't think he would be coming home.

The following day, Charlotte again secured the services of a driver and headed back to Weston-super-Mare, this time taking Parson's baby with her and also her next-door neighbour, Mrs Lucy Ostler, with whom she had become firm friends. This time, she was more fortunate. Priscilla Loveridge was at home and she and her mother were shown the baby, which bore a strong resemblance to its father, Leonard Parsons.

On 10 December, Frederick Bryant was again stricken with a mystery illness. Working in a stone quarry on the farm, he suddenly doubled over with stomach pain. Having been sick on the grass, he was sent home to recover and, according to one of his workmates, appeared to be dragging his feet as he walked.

He was attended by Dr Tracey who, on examination, found him to be suffering from the symptoms of shock, with a temperature that was well below normal. A seemingly unconcerned Charlotte told the doctor that her husband had suffered similar attacks in the past.

On 20 December, an insurance salesman, Edward Tuck, called at the Bryant's cottage hoping to sell Fred a life insurance policy. One look at the weakened, haggard man was sufficient for Tuck to decide not to proceed with the sale. Later that very day, Fred collapsed again and the Bryant's daughter, Lily, was sent to a neighbour for help. The neighbour, Mr Priddle, accompanied her back to the cottage where he found Fred vomiting profusely, groaning and writhing in agony. Byant asked for some water, but was unable to keep it down. When Charlotte put her husband's illness down to overeating, Priddle took matters into his own hands and telephoned for a doctor himself.

Dr McCarthy saw Bryant on 21 December and made up a prescription for medicine, which Charlotte was to collect from Sherborne that afternoon. Charlotte was away from home for three hours, during which time neighbours cared for Fred. He complained of awful pain, which he described as burning him inside like a red-hot poker and was convinced that he was going to die. When Charlotte returned, she unsympathetically remarked to a neighbour that it was a pity that she hadn't got him insured, saying that at least he could have a military funeral.

Fred received his first dose of medicine at six o'clock that evening, but said that it tasted foul. The medicine was promptly discarded and Fred spent an uncomfortable night in bed with his wife. Mrs Ostler also stayed overnight, sleeping on a pull out bed in the same room.

By morning, Fred's condition had worsened considerably. He had vomiting and diarrhoea and was so weak that he was unable to raise himself from the bed. Dr McCarthy was called and arrived at noon when, finding Bryant now gravely ill, he arranged for his admission to the Yeatman Hospital in Sherborne. It was there that thirty-nine-year-old Frederick Bryant died in agony just a few hours later. The doctor was at his bedside and it occurred to him that Bryant's symptoms were exactly those of arsenic poisoning. He refused to issue a death certificate.

A post-mortem examination was conducted the next day. Charlotte Bryant and Mrs Ostler visited the hospital to collect a death certificate, but once again it was refused. There would have to be an inquest, Charlotte was told.

Charlotte was not sure what this procedure involved but Mrs Ostler explained that 'they must have found something in his body which didn't ought to be there.' On their way home, the two women bumped into Edward Tuck, the insurance agent, who gallantly offered to drive them back to Coombe. During the journey, Tuck was struck by Charlotte's conversation. 'They can't say *I* poisoned him', she stated repeatedly, emphasizing the 'I'. 'I've been a good wife to him and nobody can say I haven't.'

The inquest opened on 24 December but was adjourned over Christmas. When it reopened on 27 December, a second post-mortem examination was ordered and Frederick Bryant's internal organs were sealed in jars and sent to Home Office analyst Dr Roche Lynch for testing.

Meanwhile, Dorset police began an intensive search at the Bryant's cottage. The investigating officers, led by Chief Inspector Alex Bell and Detective Sergeant Tapsell, sent Charlotte and her five children to the public assistance institution at Sturminster Newton, where she was shortly joined by her neighbour Lucy Ostler and her seven children.

With the widow Bryant and her children out of the way, numerous bottles, tins and items of clothing were removed from the cottage for testing. The floors were swept and the dust was collected. The Bryants' cat, dog, chickens and pigeons were put to sleep so that their bodies could be analysed. While police were conducting their search, a puppy from the farm on which the cottage stood died suddenly and unexpectedly. It, too, was subjected to a post-mortem examination but no connection could be found between its death and that of Fred Bryant.

Charlotte and her children were interviewed, as were Lucy Ostler and other neighbours. However, police were initially unable to trace Leonard Parsons in spite of sending cars to search large areas of Dorset, Somerset and Devon.

View of Sherborne.

The report from Dr Roche Lynch had, as expected, confirmed that Frederick Bryant had died from arsenic poisoning, so the investigating officers broadened their search to check the registers of every chemist's shop in the area. They also visited glove factories at Yeovil, where red arsenic was commonly used in the tanning of animal skins. Two particular chemist's shops attracted their attention. One in Sherborne had recorded a purchase of poison at the end of April 1935, just a few days before Bryant's initial bout of sickness. The second, in Yeovil, had sold a tin of weed killer on 21 December, the day on which Charlotte was absent from home for three hours on the pretext of collecting Fred's medicine.

By now, police had both Charlotte Bryant and Lucy Ostler in custody as prime suspects for the murder of Frederick Bryant. An identity parade was arranged in which the Yeovil chemist tried to pick out the woman who had bought poison from his shop shortly before Fred's death, signing the register with a cross. He was unable to identify either Charlotte or Lucy as his customer.

Both women had consistently denied any knowledge of the cause of Fred's death. However, it must have dawned on Lucy Ostler that she was under threat of prosecution for his murder as she asked to make another statement.

This time, Lucy gave a version of events that directly conflicted with Charlotte's statement. She told the police that, on the night that she had stayed at the cottage to assist with Bryant's nursing care, she had woken at 3 a.m. to hear Charlotte coaxing her reluctant husband to take a drink of meat extract. Shortly afterwards, she had heard him vomiting and, within twelve hours, he was dead. Charlotte had told officers that she had been so exhausted that she had slept through the night without waking. In fact, Lucy Ostler had mentioned the next morning that she had got up several times during the night to give Fred Bryant a drink of water – Charlotte maintained that she hadn't heard a thing.

In her second statement, Lucy also told police that, soon after Bryant's death, Charlotte had pointed to a tin in the cupboard saying, 'I must get rid of that'. Lucy's description of the tin matched that of the Eureka brand weed killer that the Yeovil chemist had sold to the unidentified woman. A few days later, Lucy had found the burned remains of a tin of a similar size in the ashes under the Bryant's boiler. She had thrown the ashes into the yard.

After revising her statement, Lucy Ostler was released from custody and, on 10 February 1936, Charlotte Bryant was formally charged with administering poison to her husband Frederick John Bryant and wilfully murdering him. She denied the charge.

At Sherborne Police Court, she was eventually committed for trial at the next Dorset Assizes. Prior to her hearing before the magistrates, she was permitted to see her children for the first time in weeks, playing with them for an hour or so in an anteroom.

Chralotte Bryant's trial opened before Mr Justice MacKinnon at Dorchester on 27 May 1936. Immediately, Solicitor-General Sir Terence O'Connor KC, for the prosecution, addressed the court, telling the jury that this would not be a case in which he could say that on a certain day, at a certain place, the accused woman went and bought some arsenic and took it home before putting it in her husband's tea, milk or whatever. Much of the evidence against her was circumstantial, but nevertheless strong.

Nobody was in any doubt that Frederick Bryant died as a result of the administration of arsenic and his wife had a motive for wanting him dead, that motive being Leonard Parsons. O'Connor pointed out that the one weakness in the evidence against Charlotte was that nobody had been able to show that she had ever purchased poison.

Among the first witnesses to testify were various neighbours of the Bryants who spoke of attending Fred during his bouts of sickness, including Lucy Ostler who stated that she had heard Charlotte say several times that she hated Fred.

On the second day of the trial, Leonard Parsons was called to the witness stand and caused some consternation in court when he was unable to understand the questions put to him about the nature of his relationship with the accused. Asked on what terms he was with Mrs Bryant, Parsons simply looked blank. O'Connor rephrased the question. 'Have you been intimate with Mrs Bryant?'

'I cannot understand', responded Parsons.

O'Connor tried again. 'Did you live with her as man and wife?'

'No', replied Parsons promptly.

In the end, O'Connor was forced to ask his question in much baser terms, which Parsons finally understood. 'Oh, yes', he replied enthusiastically, going on to say that he had enjoyed sexual relations with Charlotte from 1933 to 1935, something that Charlotte had consistently denied in her statements to the police.

Parsons told the court that Charlotte had wanted to marry him and that, more than once, she had asked if he would marry her were she to be widowed. According to Parsons, his answer had always been no.

Parsons denied that he had once taken a bottle into the Bryant household, the contents of which fizzled when poured onto a stone. He also spoke of trying – and failing – to buy arsenic to use in the treatment of a sick mare. He was refused the poison at the chemist's shop in Sherborne because he was not known to the proprietor. He had even applied to the police to be allowed to purchase a small quantity of arsenic, but had been turned down.

Insurance agent Edward Tuck spoke of meeting Charlotte Bryant in 1934 and being told by her that she would like to insure her 'old man'. Having called at the cottage and seen how ill Frederick looked, Tuck didn't pursue the sale any further. However, he did tell the court of giving Charlotte Bryant and Lucy Ostler a ride home from the hospital and of Charlotte's strange remarks on that occasion about poisoning.

Dr Roche Lynch gave evidence about the scientific tests he had conducted, both on Frederick Bryant's internal organs and on items removed from the cottage. He stated that, when presented with Bryant's organs for testing, they showed a remarkable degree of preservation, something that was characteristic of ingestion of arsenic. The poison was present in every organ tested and, in total, he estimated that the body contained 4.09 grains of arsenic, the normal lethal dose being between two and four grains. Furthermore, the concentration of arsenic in the dead man's fingernails suggested that the poison had been administered over a period of time, rather than as a single dose.

Roche was then cross questioned by Joshua Casswell, counsel for the defence. While conceding that, of the 146 items taken from the Bryant's cottage, 114 were found to contain no arsenic at all, Roche went on to say that the concentration of arsenic in the ashes from the Bryant's boiler was so abnormally high that something containing the poison had to have been burned there. He denied Casswell's suggestion that Bryant might have been accidentally poisoned, having eaten without washing his hands after he had been dipping sheep.

The following day, Charlotte Bryant herself took the stand. 'I cannot tell you poison' [sic], she stated firmly, while clutching the Bible tightly in her hands. 'I never had any weed killer in the house'.

On the fourth day of the trial, the jury retired, returning after an hour with a verdict of 'Guilty'. Mr Justice MacKinnon asked if Charlotte had anything to say before he passed judgement upon her.

'I am not guilty, sir, not guilty', she told him.

As sentence of death was passed upon her, Charlotte let out a long, pitiful moan. 'Not guilty' she said again, before collapsing in tears in the dock. She was half carried away from the court, her loud sobbing being heard long after she left the courtroom.

When counsel for the defence, Mr Casswell, returned to his London office on the following Monday, after having enjoyed a short holiday with his family, he found a letter awaiting him, with a further copy of the same letter sent to his home address.

'If I am right in supposing that you were the defending counsel in the case which ended at Dorchester Assizes on Saturday last', the letter read, 'would you please communicate with me as soon as possible because I have something to put before you arising out of that part of the evidence in the judge's summing up relating to the normal percentage of arsenic in coal ashes . . . ' The letter continued in a similar vein and was signed by Professor William A. Bone of the Imperial College of Science and Technology.

Casswell immediately made contact with Professor Bone and received a second letter from him, in which Bone claimed that Dr Roche Lynch's evidence on the normal proportions of arsenic found in domestic fires was seriously flawed.

It was an established fact, wrote Bone, that the normal arsenic content of house coal was not less than 140 parts to the million and, more usually, around 1,000 parts to the million. Lynch had stated in court that the ashes from the Bryant's boiler had contained 149 parts of arsenic to the million and, rather than being unusually high and suggesting that something containing arsenic had been burned there, the arsenic content was substantially less than might normally have been expected, suggesting evidence to the contrary.

Having obtained a written statement from the professor, Casswell immediately appealed the conviction, adding that he would be taking the unusual step of asking Professor Bone to appear before the Court of Appeal so that they could hear for themselves what he had to say. The hearing was fixed for 10 July and Casswell was heartened when contacted by the Solicitor-General, who told him, 'Lynch has made a dreadful blunder'.

However, any optimism that Casswell might have felt was dashed by the Lord Chief Justice, Lord Hewart, who dismissed the appeal and flatly refused even to listen to Professor Bone, who was waiting outside the court of appeal to testify.

Questions were quickly asked in Parliament about whether the Home Secretary, Sir John Simon, would consider introducing legislation to ensure that any verdict reached on mistaken evidence should be subject to inquiry on appeal. Caswell, sitting in the Stranger's Gallery of the House of Commons, was astounded by Simon's reply.

Referring specifically to the case of *Rex v. Bryant*, Simon assured the house that both the appeal judges and the trial judge were of the opinion that Professor Bone's information did not affect the validity of the jury's verdict and that, even if Lynch's evidence were wrong, the remaining evidence against Charlotte Bryant was so strong that it could be conclusively determined that no miscarriage of justice had occurred.

No one had told Charlotte Bryant of the desperate efforts to secure a reprieve on her behalf, since her defence counsel did not want to get her hopes up. Hence, she remained confined in the condemned cell, where, for the first time in her life, she learned the rudiments of reading and writing. Shortly before her execution, she made a will in which she left the sum of 5s 8½d to be divided equally between her five children. It was the first ever document that she signed with her own name rather than with her mark.

She had made one final effort to secure a reprieve of her death sentence, sending a telegram to the new king, Edward VIII. 'Mighty King. Have pity on your lowly, afflicted subject. Don't let them kill me on Wednesday'. Unfortunately for Charlotte, the Home Secretary felt unable to advise the King to spare her life and she was executed at Exeter Prison on 15 July 1936.

At the time of her execution, a Mrs Van der Elst from Kensington, a notorious campaigner for the abolition of capital punishment, drove up to the prison in her car and allegedly broke through a cord, which was barring one of the entrances. She was promptly arrested and charged with causing a breach of the peace and obstructing a police officer in the course of his duty. Magistrates dismissed the first charge against her and fined her the sum of £5 for the second. Mrs Van der Elst paid her fine and, at the same time, handed over an equal amount as a donation to the police sports fund. She announced her intentions of starting a fund, with £50,000 of her own money, to provide for the children of people who had been murdered or executed, and added that she planned to take care of Charlotte Bryant's children and pay for their education and upbringing. In the event, after Charlotte's death, the Dorset Public Assistance Committee formally adopted her five children.

20

'EVERYONE WILL BE ASTOUNDED'

Poole, 1939

Walter Alfred Dinnivan was a self-made man. Having started his working life as a coachman in Branksome Park, Poole, he went on to start a business hiring out horses and carriages. A forward thinking man, he soon recognised the potential of the motorcar, developing a profitable sideline, which eventually superseded his livery trade. He turned his business into a garage and also introduced the motor hearse to Poole.

Having prospered in business, Dinnivan invested his profits wisely and, by the 1930s, had amassed a considerable property portfolio, which included a number of flats and houses and a site at County Gates, which eventually became the Hants and Dorset bus station.

However, Dinnivan's success in business was tempered by tragedy in his personal life. In the late 1930s he lost both his wife and his only son, and, by 1939, he was sharing a flat in Poole Road, Branksome, with Hilda, his eighteen-year-old granddaughter, who took care of the cooking and housework.

On 20 May 1939, Dinnivan was to receive a visit from his grandson, Walter Dinnivan junior. Walter served in the Royal Navy as a telegrapher and had returned to England on leave after a period of duty on HMS *Suffolk*, which had taken him to China. Dinnivan met his grandson in the evening and, the following day, the two spent some time together playing darts at Westbourne Conservative Club, where Dinnivan senior was a founder member and former president and vice-president.

After he returned home to his flat, Hilda and Walter were aware of their grandfather taking a telephone call, although they were unable to hear any of the conversation, and

Branksome, 1946.

Poole Road, Branksome, 2008. Dinnivan's flat is located behind the tall hedge on the left. (© N. Sly)

he did not tell them who had called. He also made a withdrawal of around £25 from his bank account.

That evening, Hilda and Walter went out together to a dance, leaving their grandfather at home alone in the flat. At about nine o'clock in the evening, Miss Lancefield, the resident of the flat above, was sitting writing letters when she heard a thump from the flat below, then murmuring sounds, followed by silence. Fifteen minutes later, she was disturbed by a further noise, which she described as like the sound of somebody beating a carpet.

Worried, she went upstairs to rouse Miss Young who lived in the second floor flat, and both women thought that they could hear the sound of somebody breathing heavily. Nervously, the two ladies went downstairs and looked through the windows of Dinnivan's ground floor flat. The gas fire was burning in the living room and they could see nothing out of the ordinary. They noticed that Dinnivan's two cars were in his garage and wrongly presumed that his grandchildren were at home.

When Walter and Hilda returned at eleven o'clock, they found the door to the flat locked and assumed that their grandfather had gone out. They waited outside for his return for a few minutes, before walking around the house, peering through the windows. To their horror, by the light of the fire, they saw the old man lying on the carpet. Walter quickly smashed a window to gain entry and the two hurried to help their grandfather. They found him face down on the living room floor, his grey hair matted with blood and a large bloodstain on the carpet by his head.

Hilda hurriedly called the police, telling them that her grandfather had been shot. An ambulance was summoned, arriving at about half past eleven and rushing the sixty-four-year-old man to Boscombe Hospital, where he died soon afterwards without regaining consciousness.

A post-mortem examination, carried out by Home Office pathologist Sir Bernard Spilsbury, revealed that Dinnivan hadn't been shot but had been savagely attacked with a blunt instrument. His skull bore at least ten round impressions, each about three-quarters of an inch in diameter, which Spilsbury concluded had been caused by a hammer or spanner with a circular head. In addition, Dinnivan had a broken nose and two broken ribs, probably caused by someone kneeling on his chest. Marks on his neck also suggested that an attempt had been made to strangle him.

Spilsbury gave the cause of Dinnivan's death as injury to the brain and blood loss from multiple head injuries. Having examined the room in which the injured man was found, and noted extensive blood staining on his armchair and also on the back of his jacket, Spilsbury put together the most likely sequence of events on the night of 21 May. He believed that Dinnivan was sitting in the chair when the first blow was struck. The presence of bruising to the wound on the top of the victim's head indicated that he had been alive and sitting in the chair for several minutes after the initial attack. He had then moved, or been moved, after which his attacker had tried unsuccessfully to strangle him, before finally striking him several more times with the hammer. The fact that the subsequent blows were mainly to his forehead would indicate that he was probably lying down when they were struck.

To the police, robbery initially seemed the obvious motive for the attack on the elderly man. Dinnivan's wallet was missing, as were several items of valuable jewellery, including two gold rings and the silver watch that he had been wearing when his grandchildren left the house. The safe in the bedroom had been opened and emptied of bank notes and the late Mrs Dinnivan's jewellery. Whoever had opened the safe had not forced it, but had used its proper key. However, as police began to investigate the murder, they heard rumours that Dinnivan had a secret life – one about which even the granddaughter who shared his home was unaware.

Apparently, Walter Dinnivan frequently engaged the services of a prostitute, 'Miss Parsons', who called regularly at his flat. Soon, police were engaged in interviewing a number of 'women of a certain class', since Dinnivan allegedly had similar arrangements with 'Mrs Jones', 'Mrs Marlow', 'Betty', 'Gladys', 'Blondie' and 'Frenchie Lye'. According to neighbours, the visitors would enter the flat by a back entrance, via a secret passage leading from a garage in a nearby quiet road. The blinds would be drawn down, and then, a while later, the women would leave as secretly as they had arrived. On learning this, the police began to question whether the real motive might have been jealousy or blackmail and the robbery staged to throw them off the track, although after further investigation they conceded that Dinnivan's alleged use of prostitutes had been greatly exaggerated.

The local police sought help from Scotland Yard and Chief Inspector Leonard Burt soon arrived to assist them in their hunt for the killer. Burt's first action was to initiate a search for the murder weapon and also for Dinnivan's front door key, which was missing. The grounds of Dinnivan's flat were subjected to a fingertip search, which then spread out to encompass grass verges, parks and gardens within a one-mile radius. Drains and streams were also searched and two members of the public handed in hammers that they had found, but neither proved to be the one the police were seeking. Neither the key nor the weapon were ever located.

As well as investigating the possible connection with prostitutes, police were also anxious to find out who had made the telephone call to Walter Dinnivan on the morning of his attack. They appealed to the public for sightings of any suspicious people or vehicles near to his flat and were rewarded with reports of several cars and taxis seen in the area on the relevant evening, including one by a neighbour, Mr Smith, who had seen two men speeding away from the scene in a black car. In addition, Dinnivan's flat was found to contain items that may have been left behind by his attacker.

On a table in the centre of the living room were two glasses, a whisky tumbler and a beer glass, with a beer bottle. Both of the glasses and the bottle had been tipped onto their sides and some of the beer had spilled onto the tablecloth. Dinnivan had never been known to drink beer and the glass bore a thumbprint that wasn't his, nor had any other members of the family left it. In addition, the police found the dog ends of four cigarettes, each smoked right down to the cork tip. One lay on the tablecloth near the glasses, two more were found under the table and the fourth was found on the settee. Dinnivan himself smoked un-tipped cigarettes. On the floor was a woman's French hair curler of a most unusual design. It was made from imitation tortoiseshell and the celluloid used in its manufacture was so flammable that its sale had been banned in England because of the risk of fire. Finally, police retrieved a brown paper bag from the flat. It was bloodstained and had been folded on the diagonal.

Police officers travelled far and wide in their hunt for Dinnivan's killer. They went to London in search of those prostitutes who regularly came from the capital to sparsely populated areas such as Dorset because they felt that the risk of arrest was smaller. They spoke to Dinnivan's friends, relatives and business associates, as well as the taxi drivers and shopkeepers from the area and, before long, they felt that they had come up with a plausible suspect.

Local man Joseph Williams was a former Army officer, who had now fallen on hard times. Having separated from his wife in 1937 and moved in with another woman, Williams had taken out a large mortgage in order to buy two properties. However, in 1938 his business had failed and his partner had left him. His wife had returned and the couple had lived for a while in a boarding house before moving to one of the two houses in Ingworth Road, Branksome. He had defaulted on the mortgage payments and, in spite of selling almost all his possessions, was on the verge of eviction, an order having been granted to the building society for repossession by Poole County Court on 10 May 1939. By the time police arrived to interview him, Williams was living in a single room, with only a camp bed, chair and table for furniture.

Williams had known Dinnivan for more than fifty years and had often borrowed money from him in the past, the last occasion being when Dinnivan had loaned him £5 only a few days before his death. Williams told police that he had last seen his old friend on 14 May and again on either 16 or 17 May. On the first meeting, Williams had told Dinnivan of his imminent eviction and suggested that he buy the property from the building society, but Dinnivan had not been interested. On the second occasion, Dinnivan had invited Williams to his flat for a drink, loaned him £5 and showed him his wife's jewellery.

On the night of the murder, Williams told police that he had been at home until about 8.30 p.m., only popping out for five minutes to buy cigarettes. At 9.30 p.m. he had walked into Bournemouth, hearing a clock strike 10 p.m. as he reached the square. After strolling round the pier and Pine Walk, he had caught a bus home, arriving at 11.30 p.m., after which he had gone to bed.

Williams was arrested on 20 June 1939. His response to being charged with the murder of Walter Dinnivan was incredulity. 'The whole thing is ridiculous', he said. 'Everyone will be astounded'. He was remarkably unfazed by his circumstances, smiling cheerily at the press photographers as he left the police station en route to Poole magistrate's court and chatting about his intentions to attend a whist drive that evening as he waited in court for the arrival of the magistrates.

Williams pleaded 'Not Guilty' and his defence counsel argued eloquently on his behalf. King pointed out the danger of Dinnivan's lifestyle and the frequent visitors to his flat, who were able to come and go through a concealed entrance without being observed. King maintained that Williams was a sick man who, at the age of seventy, was now facing the most serious charge it was possible for anyone to face. The arguments failed to sway the magistrates, who determined that there was a case to answer, committing Williams to stand trial at the next Assizes in Dorchester.

Joseph Williams under arrest.
(Daily Echo, Bournemouth)

The trial opened on 11 October before Mr Justice Croom-Johnson. J.D. Casswell prosecuted, while J.G. Trapnell KC led the defence.

Although he again pleaded 'Not Guilty', the weight of evidence against Williams seemed insurmountable to his defence counsel. Penniless and facing imminent eviction and homelessness, he certainly had the motive to rob his old friend, who he knew to be a wealthy man. Money found in his wallet after the murder, which Williams claimed to have won on the horses, was traced back to Dinnivan's branch of Lloyds Bank. The thumbprint on the beer glass was identical to Williams's and, in a ground-breaking forensic test, the saliva from the cork-tipped cigarettes was found to come from someone with blood group number 3, the same group as Williams. It was a particularly rare blood group, shared by only 5 per cent of the population.

Having checked 130 outlets in Bournemouth and Poole, police had conclusively established that the French hair curler was not available for sale anywhere in the area. Yet Mrs Williams used identical curlers. The bloodstained brown paper bag was found to have a fault in the serrations on its edge and no less than twenty-three similar bags were found in Williams's room, each with a similar fault and all obviously manufactured by the same machine. The police were able to establish that Williams had bought a job lot of the bags from a shop that was closing down.

Casswell outlined the prosecution's theory about the murder. Destitute and desperate, Williams had visited Dinnivan with the intention of robbing him. As the two men enjoyed a drink, Williams had removed the hammer he had brought with him from its paper bag and hit Dinnivan hard from behind on the top of the head, rendering him unconscious. Then, as Williams was rifling through the safe, either he heard the two ladies from the upstairs flats or Dinnivan had regained consciousness. It had then been necessary to kill him, to prevent him from later identifying his attacker.

On the third day of the trial – Friday 13 October – Williams himself took the stand and it was at that moment that the case went wrong for the prosecution team.

Casswell would later write in his memoirs, *A Lance for Liberty*, that Mr Justice Croom-Johnson appeared extremely prejudiced for the defendant, almost as if he were reluctant to put on the traditional black cap and pronounce a death sentence. Casswell believed that this was the first murder case that Croom-Johnson had presided over, and whether he was suffering from first-time nerves or just particularly sympathetic to the age of the accused, it soon became evident to Casswell that he was fighting an uphill battle.

As Casswell cross-examined Williams, Croom-Johnson fidgeted, snorted and exclaimed loudly from the bench, while Williams rather cockily proceeded to argue every piece of the evidence against him that the police had gathered. He denied being anywhere near Dinnivan's flat when the murder was committed and explained the presence of his thumbprint on the beer glass by suggesting that it had been improperly washed after his previous visit on 14 May. He could have left the curler on another occasion and he wasn't the only person in the area with a rare blood group. As for the paper bag – surely anyone from that area might have received one of the defective ones from the local shop?

As soon as Casswell had finished his cross-examination, Croom-Johnson immediately invited the jury to dismiss the case there and then. 'You have heard this man and seen him in the box', he told them. 'Recollect that the prosecution has to establish a case for your satisfaction without any reasonable doubt and, having regard to the fact that none of the money has really been traced to this man and no bloodstains, with the exception of those on a pair of trousers, have been found on any of his clothing, if you think that this case is one in which it would be unsafe to leave him in peril any longer you are at liberty to say so but if you think the case ought to proceed you are also at liberty to say so.' After a five-minute recess, the jury elected to continue the trial but Croom-Johnson had not finished interfering.

In his summing up, Croom-Johnson again seemed to bend over backwards to refute the case for the prosecution. He reminded the jury that the murder weapon had never been found, in spite of an extensive search and that none of the missing jewellery had been traced. He ridiculed the hair curler, asking if a woman's hair curler were really the sort of thing that a murderer took along with him to the scene of the crime. He pointed out that there were approximately 15,000 people in the Bournemouth district with the same blood group as Williams and that there was no evidence that he smoked, or ever bought, cork-tipped cigarettes. He finished his summing up by instructing the jury that, while it was proper that they should punish the guilty, it was better that dozens of guilty persons should escape rather than one innocent person suffer wrongly. They should be quite certain in their minds that they were not convicting the wrong person.

Within seventy minutes, the jury had returned a verdict of 'Not Guilty' and an obviously delighted Joseph Williams was a free man. He was whisked away from the court by Norman Rae of the *News of the World*, to whom he had promised an exclusive interview. Frustratingly for Rae, he subsequently found himself with not just a story, but with a journalistic scoop, but one that he was forced by journalistic ethics to withhold for twelve years until after William's death in 1951.

Initially, Williams maintained his innocence to Rae, saying that he had known all along that he wouldn't be convicted and had therefore taken a perverse pleasure in playing the police along, amusing himself at their efforts to tie him to the murder. However, after a long evening of celebratory drinking, Rae found Williams knocking at the door of his hotel room in the early hours of the morning.

In tears, Williams told Rae that he needed to clear his conscience. 'The jury were wrong', he confessed. 'It was me. I killed Walter Dinnivan. Now I've told you, I feel better. I'll be able to sleep now.'

Rae escorted Williams back to his own room then lay awake mulling over what he had just been told. In the eyes of the law, having been tried and acquitted, Joseph Williams could not be tried again for the same offence. No matter what statements he might make after the trial, he was officially innocent and could not now be brought to justice.

By morning, Williams had recovered from the excesses of the night before and was now openly bragging about how he had avoided the hangman. Rae kept in touch with him for a few years but eventually lost track of him until the beginning of March 1951, when Williams died penniless and alone in Nottingham. Only then was Rae free to reveal his story, but since Williams's confession was only hearsay, the case of the murder of Walter Dinnivan could not be officially closed.

[Note: In certain contemporary accounts of the murder, the victim's name is alternatively spelled Dinivan. I have taken the spelling used by the majority.]

21

'THIS IS MY NIGHT TO HOWL'

Dorchester, 1941

David Miller Jennings was, it was said, the stuff of which heroes are made. Recognising that war was inevitable, Jennings, a former miner and farm labourer from Warrington, had joined the Army in 1938, determined to fight for King and country. He had seen action in Dunkirk and generally conducted himself with courage and dignity, but tragically his actions were to cause the death of another equally courageous and dignified soldier; in this instance, one who had fought in the trenches during the First World War.

On 26 January 1941, twenty-year-old Jennings, now stationed at Dorchester, had been for a training session on the rifle range. Yet shooting at targets had failed to ease the anger and bitterness he felt at having recently received a 'Dear John' letter from the girl he loved and had fully expected to marry. That evening, in the company of a number of his comrades, Jennings tried to drown his sorrows with drink.

Their evening started with several pints of beer, alternated by shots of whisky, at the George Hotel. From there the group moved to the Antelope Hotel, where they drank yet more beer and whisky, then to the Ship Inn. There, Corporal Leith spotted him buying a round of drinks.

Leith had good reason to be surprised since Jennings, who was spending freely on drinks, owed him money. He tapped Jennings on the shoulder and remarked to him, 'That five shillings you borrowed off me seems to be going a long way.'

Jennings smiled drunkenly at him. 'I borrowed more, Corp.' he explained. 'This is my night to howl.'

The barracks at Dorchester.

High West Street, Dorchester, 1946.

'Then make sure you don't end up howling in the guardroom', Leith warned him.

Shortly afterwards, Leith shook his head as he watched Jennings and his companions stagger out of the bar. Aware that Jennings had been jilted, Leith was of the opinion that he was now spending the money he had carefully saved in anticipation of his marriage.

The drinkers returned to the Antelope Hotel where Jennings bought yet more beer. At closing time the group moved to a milk bar, where they ate meat pies and drank cups of tea, before making their way unsteadily back to barracks.

During the course of the evening, Jennings had consumed around seven shots of whisky and ten and a half pints of beer. His friends described him as 'talkative and merry', but by the time they reached their rooms the reality of his situation was slowly beginning to dawn on Jennings. Not only had he lost his girl but also he had just spent all his savings on drink. Furthermore, he still owed money to Corporal Leith and others.

Private Hall, with whom he shared a room, watched in disbelief as Jennings stripped off his best battle dress and, instead of changing into his pyjamas, put on his second-best battle dress with a pair of gym shoes. 'What the hell are you up to, David?' asked Hall.

'Nothing', replied Jennings brusquely.

'It has to be something otherwise you'd be putting on your pyjamas instead of that bloody lot. Come off it – what are you on?'

'If you must know, I'm going to do a break in', said Jennings.

Hall tried his hardest to dissuade him, but was told by Jennings to mind his own business. Hall redoubled his efforts to stop Jennings when he saw him pick up his rifle and take some ammunition from his bandolier.

'Leave that. You're too jerked up to take a rifle with you.'

Jennings ignored him. 'Don't you split on me', he warned Hall who, knowing the unspoken Army code of not ratting on your pals, eventually decided that he had tried hard enough. He fell asleep as Jennings crept quietly out of their room.

Jennings managed to leave the barracks without being seen and walked into Dorchester. Meanwhile, Corporal Leith was becoming increasingly concerned about the young private, so much so that he decided to go to his room to check on his welfare.

'Where is he?' he asked the sleepy Hall. When he failed to get a sensible response from Jennings's roommate, Leith walked over to Jennings's bed where the young soldier had discarded the bandolier. Leith picked it up and quickly counted the rounds. It should have contained fifty rounds, but now ten were missing.

In Prince's Street in Dorchester, garage owner Jesse Broughton was awakened by the sound of four loud bangs. He peered out of his window, but saw nothing and so returned to his bed. What he didn't realise was that the noises he had heard were shots coming from the office below his bedroom. Jennings had broken into the office and tried unsuccessfully to shoot his way into the safe there.

In wartime England, the sound of bumps in the night was not unusual and Broughton got back into bed, ready to resume his sleep. Minutes later, as his clock struck a quarter past midnight, he heard six rifle shots – five loud cracks, followed by a pause of about thirty seconds, then a further crack. Seconds later, someone ran past his house, clicking a rifle bolt as they passed.

Prince's Street, Dorchester, 2008. (© R. Sly)

Shortly afterwards, David Jennings ran into the barrack room, slamming the door closed behind him. Blood dripped from several cuts on his face. Corporal Leith witnessed his return and went straight to the barrack room. When Leith got there, Jennings had his back against the door, forcing Leith to shoulder the door open and push past him.

'Where have you been? What have you been doing, soldier?' asked Leith.

Jennings was still breathless from running, but managed to reply that he had just broken into the NAAFI and that he thought he might have shot a man.

Leith seized and checked Jennings's rifle, finding it empty then marched the young man down to the guardroom, where he was searched and locked up. Jennings had absolutely no money on him. Next, Leith went in search of another officer and, finding Sergeant Murch, told him what he knew and asked the sergeant to accompany him to the NAAFI on Prince's Street in Dorchester.

The first thing that the two men noticed on their arrival was a strong smell of gas. They surmised that Jennings had shot and ruptured a gas pipe and, conscious of the strict wartime blackout regulations, Leith switched on his torch and, carefully shielding the beam, swung it around until he found the fractured gas pipe.

The lock had been shot from the back door and, although it wouldn't open fully, the officers were able to enter the darkened building without any problems. They were barely inside, when Murch suddenly tripped. Leith lowered the torch beam to illuminate the floor and saw that his companion had stumbled over the body of an elderly man, lying by the door. With Leith continuing to light his way, Murch squatted to check the old man, finding that he had been shot and was dead. The civil police were immediately sent for.

The victim was Albert Edward Farley, aged sixty-five, who had just that very day started his new job as night watchman at the NAAFI, after retiring from his profession as a tailor. The veteran of the First World War had found retirement tedious and was eagerly anticipating his return to work. Under normal circumstances, the duties of the night watchman were not expected to be arduous and Farley would be able to sleep at his post, a camp bed being set up in the office for that very purpose. Earlier that evening, Bert had been joking with the canteen manageress about getting paid to sleep. Now, just a few short hours later, he would never wake again.

A post-mortem examination, conducted by Dr G.O. Taylor, would later show that Farley had been shot just below his heart by a bullet fired from a service rifle. The bullet had been fired at a downward angle and had exited Mr Farley's back four inches below the entrance wound, just to the right of his spine. Dr Taylor was unable to establish from which direction the rifle was fired, as he was unsure of the victim's exact position when he was hit. However, he was able to determine that the shot had not been fired from close range

Police Sergeant Lill arrived to interview David Jennings at the barracks at 5.40 a.m. Still very drunk, Jennings made several rambling and contradictory statements but curiously at no time did he ever deny the possibility that he might have shot a man. It took several hours before Sergeant Lill was able to get a sufficiently coherent response from Jennings but, as soon as he had made and signed his statement, he was arrested and charged with Farley's murder. He was taken to the police station and from there to the magistrate's court, where the pressure of the constant questioning finally got to him. In tears, he buried his face in his hands and was heard to exclaim, 'Oh, my God!'

In order for a man to be charged with murder, there has to be evidence of intent. In other words, a murderer has to intend to actually kill his victim and it was extremely unlikely that David Jennings had any prior intention of killing Bert Farley. Without intent, Jennings should have been facing a manslaughter charge rather than one of murder – yet the magistrates allowed the police charge to stand and committed him to the next Dorset Assizes on a charge of murder. When one of the magistrates was later questioned about this decision, his response was to say that, 'There was a war on. We didn't have time to think of things like that.'

Jennings's trial opened before Mr Justice Charles on 3 June 1941. Mr Henderson prosecuted, while Mr Trapnell handled the defence under the auspices of the Poor Prisoner Rules, which provided counsel for defendants without the necessary means to pay for it. Jennings pleaded 'Not Guilty'.

Henderson began by trying to unravel the conflicting statements given by Jennings at the barracks in the early morning after the killing. At times, Jennings had stated, 'I shot a man', then the wording of his statement had changed to, 'I don't know whether I shot anyone.' Although Jennings had been searched by Leith on his return to the barracks and found to have no money on him, Henderson maintained that he had managed to surreptitiously pass the sum of 32s, which he had stolen from the NAAFI, onto another soldier for safekeeping.

Henderson then addressed the matter of the amount of drink that Jennings had consumed on the night of the murder. He pointed out that drunkenness was no excuse for the crime. It stood to reason that when a man used a rifle to fire at another man, there was likelihood that it might kill him. Drink could only be offered as an excuse if the shooter were so befuddled by it that he didn't know what he was doing, and there was no doubt that Jennings knew exactly what he was doing when he took his rifle and ammunition and went off to commit a robbery.

The manageress of the NAAFI gave evidence about the amount of money that had been stolen from the cash box. She was adamant that the exact sum stolen had been 37s and 6d – considerably more than the 32s that Jennings was alleged to have given the other soldier.

Jennings himself gave evidence. He admitted that he knew where the cash box was kept at the NAAFI, but didn't realise that a caretaker had been newly appointed. He had shot at the back door lock five times, then panicked and ran when he heard Farley shouting from inside. As the door to the NAAFI opened, a shaft of light appeared and Jennings turned to look at it, firing his rifle almost instinctively without aiming. His account of the shots fired was, of course, consistent with the evidence of Jesse Broughton, who had heard five reports, a pause and then a sixth.

Unfortunately, Trapnell didn't pick up on the fact that Broughton's evidence corroborated his client's version of events. Instead, he chose to focus his defence on trying to show that Jennings was incapable, due to the effects of the large quantities of alcohol he had consumed prior to the murder. He pointed out that, to return a verdict of murder, the jury must believe that the prosecution had proved malice aforethought and, if they did not believe that this had been done, then it was their duty to return a lesser verdict of manslaughter. Trapnell was of the opinion that malice aforethought had definitely not been established.

However, rather than hammering home the legalities of murder versus manslaughter to the jury, Trapnell then chose to divert his arguments back to the alcohol. He stressed to the jury that drink affects different people in different ways, saying that Jennings's crime was not a clever act carried out by a clever criminal, but a stupid, drunken escapade by a young man who had just been jilted by his girlfriend. He reminded the jury of the cuts on Jennings's face. These had been caused by splinters of metal that ricocheted off the safe that Jennings had tried to blast his way into, and Trapnell pointed out the sheer stupidity of choosing such a dangerous and noisy way of attempting to open a safe.

What Trapnell failed to capitalise upon was the evidence of Corporal Leith and Sergeant Murch. Both stated that Farley's body was positioned up against the door of the NAAFI in such a way that they had to struggle to get into the building. Even with the aid of a torch, Murch stumbled over the body in the pitch darkness. Yet, according to the prosecution, Jennings, without a torch, allegedly shot the night watchman, manoeuvred his way through the canteen in the darkness, located and emptied the cash box and found his way out of the building, managing to wedge Farley's body against the inside of the door as he left.

In his summing up of the case for the jury, Mr Justice Charles showed no sympathy for the young defendant, who had passed his twenty-first birthday while in custody awaiting his trial. He pointed out that drunkenness could not be considered an adequate defence, saying that there was no evidence that Jennings was so drunk that he was incapable of acting intentionally. On the contrary, Jennings had found himself short of money and had deliberately gone out with the intention of committing a robbery. By arming himself beforehand, he had demonstrated intent to shoot if anyone had stood in his way.

The jury had been left little option but to arrive at a verdict of guilty of murder. Nevertheless, they deliberated for two hours before reaching that verdict.

Before donning his black cap, Mr Justice Charles asked Jennings if he had anything to say before sentence was pronounced. Jennings looked the judge directly in the eye and replied, 'I did not intend to kill that man'.

Having been sentenced to death, Jennings was not without sympathisers among the general public, who felt that his recent training in violence, which enabled him to fight the enemy, had some bearing on the shooting. The people from his hometown organised a petition to appeal to the Home Office for clemency, as did the Army, and his defence counsel immediately announced his intention to appeal the conviction.

The appeal was held before the Court of Criminal Appeal on 7 July 1941 and again Trapnell argued that not enough direction had been given to the jury with regard to Jennings's state of intoxication at the time of the offence. However, the Lord Chief Justice was entirely satisfied that the judge had successfully addressed this in his summing up and the appeal was dismissed.

After the appeal failed, Captain Simon Wingfield-Digby, the then member of parliament for West Dorset, was drawn into the battle to save Private Jennings, personally contacting Home Secretary Mr Herbert Morrison. However, Morrison replied that he felt unable to commute Jennings's sentence.

George E. Chappell was next into the fray. Chappell, the prospective liberal candidate for West Dorset, shared the opinion of many that, in this instance, the law had erred. 'You and I know that His Majesty will not be unmindful of the unselfish service and sacrifice that this soldier has given to his country', he said in an address to his prospective constituents. Appealing for clemency directly to a higher authority than the Home Secretary, he sent off a carefully worded telegram to His Majesty King George VI.

Whether or not the king replied is not recorded. That he didn't choose to intervene is evident since, on 23 July 1941, Thomas Pierrepoint executed David Miller Jennings at Dorchester for the murder of Albert Edward Farley.

Had Jennings been correctly tried for manslaughter rather than murder, then he would undoubtedly have served a prison sentence and his life would have been spared. As it was, two war heroes from different generations died needlessly, the first because of a 'Dear John' letter, and the second as a result of a flawed legal decision made hurriedly because 'there was a war on'.

22

'PUT ME DOWN AS NOT GUILTY, OLD BOY'

London & Bournemouth, 1946

Group Captain Rupert Brooke looked the very picture of respectability. Tall and broad-shouldered, he carried himself with a military bearing befitting his rank. An intelligent and well-spoken man, his fair, wavy hair and piercing blue eyes, coupled with a charming manner, ensured that he was never short of female admirers.

On 3 July 1946, he met the latest of his conquests while out for a stroll on the promenade in Bournemouth. Doreen Marshall of Pinner, Middlesex, had recently been discharged from the WRNS. Shortly afterwards, she fell ill with a bout of influenza and, deciding that some sea air would do her good, had travelled to Bournemouth to convalesce.

She was only too pleased to meet a handsome stranger and, after chatting with Brooke for some time, accepted his invitation to take tea with him at the hotel where he was staying, the Tollard Royal in West Hill Road.

She enjoyed a pleasant afternoon with her new-found friend, so much so that she agreed to return to his hotel and dine with him that evening. At first, the dinner date was enjoyable, but by the time the meal had finished, Brooke was beginning to show the effects of the alcohol he had drunk that evening and Miss Marshall was finding his company a little wearing. Looking strained, she asked another hotel resident to order her a taxi to take her back to the Norfolk Hotel on Richmond Hill. However, Brooke cancelled the taxi, promising that he would walk her back. As the couple left the Tollard Royal, he remarked to the night porter that he would be back in half an hour. 'No, in a quarter of an hour', argued Miss Marshall and the two walked off together in the direction of Richmond Hill.

Tollard Royal Hotel, Bournemouth, 1953.

The Norfolk Hotel, Bournemouth, 1950s.

By 4.30 a.m., the night porter had not seen Group Captain Brooke return. He went up to Brooke's room and quietly opened the door to see Brooke fast asleep in his bed, having apparently entered the hotel by shinning up a ladder and climbing through his bedroom window. His shoes, which would normally have been left out for cleaning, were by his bed, caked in wet sand.

The following morning, Brooke was challenged by the head porter about his unorthodox return to the hotel and insisted that he had been playing a joke on the night porter. Other residents at the hotel noticed that Brooke had some fresh scratch marks on his neck, which he had partially concealed with a scarf. He was also spending freely at the hotel bar and, unusually, paying for his drinks with cash rather than adding them to his bill.

On 5 July, the manager of the Norfolk Hotel felt sufficiently concerned about the absence of one of his guests, Miss Marshall, to telephone the police in Bournemouth and report her missing. Having done some investigating of his own, the manager subsequently rang the Tollard Royal Hotel and spoke to Brooke, asking him if his dinner guest on 3 July had been a Miss Marshall from Pinner. Brooke laughed off the idea, saying that he had known his lady friend for years and she did not come from Pinner. Nevertheless, the hotel manager concluded the conversation by advising Brooke to contact the police and later that same day Brooke did exactly that.

He telephoned the police station at Bournemouth and asked if there was a photograph of the missing woman. When told that there was, he declined the police's offer to bring the photograph to his hotel for him to look at, promising to call in at the police station instead.

When he arrived at the police station, he immediately aroused suspicion because he seemed to be dressed too casually for a high-ranking RAF officer, wearing his shirt buttoned to the neck, with no tie or cravat. As he chatted with Detective Constable George Suter about his air force service, the policeman noticed several inconsistencies in his descriptions of aircraft types. Brooke dropped his pipe at one point in the conversation and, as he bent down to retrieve it, the observant police officer spotted what looked like a fingernail mark on his neck. In addition, Suter couldn't help but notice that Brooke bore a remarkable resemblance to a wanted poster recently issued by Scotland Yard, currently pinned on the wall of the police station's CID office.

Suter excused himself for another look at the poster, bringing it back into the interview with him when he returned and confronting Brooke with the question, 'Is that you?'

Brooke glanced at the poster briefly. 'Good Lord, no!' he replied quickly, before conceding. 'But I agree it is like me.'

Brooke later met Doreen Marshall's father and sister at the police station and joked about his likeness to the wanted poster. Yet the officers at Bournemouth were not treating the resemblance quite so lightly and detained Brooke pending further enquiries.

As Brooke waited at the police station, he complained of feeling cold and asked if police could fetch his jacket from the hotel. Officers agreed, taking the opportunity to search the pockets of the jacket as they did. They recovered an artificial pearl bead, a first-class return Bournemouth-London train ticket and a ticket from the left luggage office of the Bournemouth West Station, issued on 23 June.

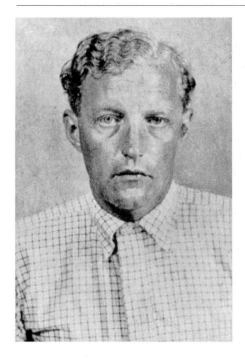

Neville Heath. (Daily Echo, Bournemouth)

When they redeemed the ticket, they were given a suitcase, which contained a bloodstained scarf and a leather-covered riding whip, with a plaited leather thong. A search of Brooke's room at the Tollard Royal later turned up a tightly knotted, bloody handkerchief, with a few hairs entangled in the knot.

At 9.45 p.m. that evening, officers informed Brooke that they were now satisfied that he was the Mr Neville George Clevely Heath wanted by Scotland Yard in connection with the murder of Margery Gardner on 20–21 June, and that he would be detained in Bournemouth pending the arrival of their colleagues from London. 'Brooke's' only comment was, 'Oh, all right.'

Later that evening, he volunteered to write a statement, giving his account of his meeting with twenty-one-year-old Doreen Marshall and another woman who he knew as Peggy. Having described eating dinner with Doreen, he told of walking her back to her hotel. According to Heath – for he had now acknowledged his true identity – the couple had chatted for at least an hour and Miss Marshall had been insistent that he needn't trouble himself to escort her all the way back to her hotel. Hence, he had left her at the entrance to Bournemouth pier, watching her cross the road and enter the gardens, before returning to his own hotel.

Some hours later, Heath offered to make a further statement, this time on the murder of Margery Gardner.

Heath and Gardner had met at the Panama Club in South Kensington, London. After an evening of drinking and dancing, thirty-two-year-old Gardner, who was known to favour masochistic sexual practices, had agreed to accompany Heath back to his room at the Pembridge Court Hotel in Notting Hill.

She was found dead in the hotel room the following morning. She had been tied up and savagely beaten, before being suffocated. Her body bore the marks of seventeen whip lashes, both her nipples had been almost completely bitten off and she had severe internal damage caused by the forceful insertion of a large object into her vagina. Of 'Lieutenant Colonel' Heath, there was no trace.

However, the following weekend, Superintendent Barratt, the officer in charge of the inquiry into Gardner's murder, received a letter from Heath. In it, he claimed to have had drinks with Margery Gardner, during which time she had told him that she was obliged to sleep with someone, Heath had assumed for financial reasons. He had offered Margery the use of his hotel room for her assignation, given her his keys and told her that he would return at 2 a.m. When he returned at 3 a.m., it was to find Miss Gardner '. . . in the condition of which you are aware'.

Realising that he would immediately be under suspicion for her murder, he had quickly packed his belongings and left. The letter continued with a description of 'Jack', Miss Gardner's friend who, according to Heath, was aged about thirty, with black hair and a small moustache, 5ft 9in tall and of medium build. It concluded with Heath writing that he had the instrument with which Miss Gardner was beaten in his possession and promising to forward it to the police. They would find his fingerprints on it, he wrote, but they would also find other prints too.

The 'instrument' never arrived and, in his new statement to Bournemouth police, Heath admitted that it was the riding whip that they had found in his suitcase. He insisted that he had not murdered Margery Gardner, although he had been present when she was killed.

Branksome Dene Chine, Bournemouth, 1930s.

Meanwhile, the police mounted an intensive search for any trace of Doreen Marshall, in the course of which they found several discarded items of clothing and pieces of jewellery. Doreen's father and sister were shown every find, but were unable to positively identify any of the items as having belonged to Doreen.

On 7 July, Kathleen Evans was walking her dog at Branksome Dene Chine when she noticed huge numbers of flies swarming round rhododendron bushes. The following day, she read a report about Doreen Marshall's disappearance in the local newspaper and asked her parents to go back with her to the spot where she had seen the clouds of insects. The search for Doreen Marshall was over.

The young woman was huddled in bushes, naked except for one shoe. Her clothes had been piled on top of her body and her stockings, powder compact and twenty-seven pearls from her broken necklace lay nearby.

The cause of her death was a deep cut across her throat but, in addition, her body had also been severely mutilated. She was covered in bruises and small cuts, and both hands were cut as if she had seized the blade of a knife while trying to fend off her attacker. She had several broken ribs, including one that had splintered and been driven into one of her lungs. Both her nipples had been bitten, the right one having been completely severed and the left severely torn. A sharp object had been thrust into her vagina and she had long, deep knife wounds across her thighs and breasts.

The following morning, Doreen's handbag was found behind beach huts at Durley Chine. A diamond ring and a fob watch were also recovered, having been sold to a shop in Bournemouth soon after she had disappeared.

About forty yards from Doreen's body, police also found a pile of permed head hair, obviously from a woman. As Heath had made a statement in which he had admitted meeting a woman called Peggy at the same time as he had met Doreen, it was feared that they might be investigating a double murder. They intensified their search of the area, even calling in a bloodhound, but were unable to discover any further information about either the hair or the identity of the mysterious Peggy.

Heath was charged with the murders of Margery Gardner and Doreen Marshall but tried only for Gardner's murder. He was a habitual criminal who had a string of convictions for petty crimes, which began at an early age. Born in Ilford, Essex, in 1917, he was a precocious child who grew up into a self-confident, even arrogant, young man.

Having joined the RAF on a short service commission in 1936, less than a year later he faced a court martial for stealing a car belonging to an NCO, being absent without leave and escaping while under arrest. This was sufficient to earn his dismissal from the RAF in September 1937 and, two months later, he was arrested for fraudulently obtaining credit at a hotel in Nottingham, stealing a car and passing himself off as the Earl of Dudley. Eight more offences were taken into consideration and he was eventually put on probation.

Having taken a job in a shop in Oxford Street, which he kept for two weeks before being sacked, he was sentenced to three years Borstal training in July 1938 for passing a forged cheque, housebreaking and stealing from his fiancé. The onset of the Second World War precipitated his release and he was conscripted into the Army and posted to the Middle East.

By 1941, he had gone absent without leave and had also obtained a second pay book in order to draw double pay. He was again court-martialled and sent home to England aboard the troopship *Mooltan*. He jumped ship at Durban, South Africa, and, by the time he reached Johannesburg, he had become 'Captain Selway MC' of the Argyll and Sutherland Highlanders.

Having passed several forged cheques, he thought it prudent to reinvent himself yet again and thus it was 'Robert Armstrong' who enlisted in the South African Air Force, eventually rising to the rank of Captain. During his time in South Africa, 'Robert Armstrong' met and married Elizabeth Pitt-Rivers, the sixteen-year-old daughter of a prominent South African businessman. In due course Elizabeth gave birth to Robert Armstrong junior.

In 1944, Armstrong was seconded to the RAF and served with 180 Squadron, baling out of his damaged aircraft on his first flight over enemy territory. He returned to South Africa after the war's end to find that his wife had instigated divorce proceedings against him. He was cashiered from the South African Air Force, having committed a string of serious offences and returned to Britain, where, in April 1946, he was fined for impersonating an officer and wearing a uniform and medals that he was not entitled to wear. Now, just months later, he was facing the most serious charge of all.

His trial for the murder of Margery Gardner opened at the Old Bailey on 24 September 1946, before Mr Justice Morris. Mr E.A. Hawke prosecuted, with J.D. Casswell acted in Heath's defence. Heath stood rigidly to attention in the dock to enter his plea of 'Not Guilty'.

One of the first witnesses to be called against him was Yvonne Mary Symonds. The slight, dark-haired young woman was at several points close to fainting as she told of meeting Heath at a dance in Chelsea on 15 June. At the end of the following day, which they spent together, Heath proposed marriage and Yvonne accepted. That evening, they had slept together in the very hotel room in which Margery Gardner was to meet her death less than a week later.

Yvonne returned home to Worthing the following morning and, that week, received several telephone calls from her fiancé, who she met again in Worthing on 21 and 22 June. On their second meeting, Heath had asked her if she had read about a murder in the newspapers and, when she replied that she hadn't, told her that it had occurred in 'their' room at the Pembridge Court Hotel. Heath had told her that he had seen the body, describing it as a 'very gruesome sight'.

Miss Symonds testified that Heath had told her that he had lent his key to the room to another man and slept elsewhere that night, but had been contacted by the police and taken to see the body. He had told her that a poker had been 'stuck up' Margery Gardner and theorised that only a 'sexual maniac' could have done such a thing.

The following day, Yvonne Symonds had read an account of the murder in the papers and learned that the police wished to interview her fiancé. She had telephoned Heath and told him that her parents were very worried. Heath had promised to ring her that evening, but she had never spoken to him again.

Throughout the first day of the trial, the prosecution carefully avoided mentioning the murder of Doreen Marshall, since to do so would have prejudiced the case. Yet Casswell, for the defence, introduced the second murder himself as part of a preconceived plan to

The Old Bailey, London.

show that Heath was insane. He reasoned that the worse he could make Heath appear to the jury, the more likely they would be to believe that no sane man could possibly have committed such heinous acts.

The counsel for the defence had been convinced of his client's insanity since their very first meeting while Heath was incarcerated in Brixton Prison. Heath had indicated that he would probably plead guilty and Casswell had told him to think of his parents and his brother. Having considered briefly, Heath had nonchalantly conceded 'All right. Put me down as not guilty, old boy.' Life obviously meant little to Heath, and Casswell was convinced that, prior to his arrest, it had been his intention to commit suicide. He had specifically asked to be moved to a room with a gas fire at the Tollard Royal Hotel – hardly a necessity, given the summer weather – and an un-posted note to his parents had been found, written on hotel stationery, in which he talked of ending his life.

Casswell had arranged for Heath to be examined by Dr William Hubert, a doctor who not only had an impressive list of qualifications, but also a wealth of experience in working in prisons and the Broadmoor Criminal Lunatic Asylum, as it was then known. After visiting Heath several times in prison, Hubert came to the conclusion that he was not an ordinary sexual pervert who gained pleasure from unconventional sexual practices, but a person who suffered from moral insanity and was quite unaware that what he was doing was wrong. Casswell intended to show that Heath fell within the McNaghten Rules, named after Daniel McNaghten who shot and killed the prime minister's private secretary in 1843, having meant to shoot the prime minister himself. McNaghten was subsequently acquitted when a jury found that his mental state was such that he did not know the difference between right and wrong.

Accordingly, Casswell did not call Heath to the witness stand, telling the jury that they would probably not believe a word he said. Casswell was actually afraid that Heath would appear too intelligent, calm and rational – hardly the best attributes for convincing a jury of his insanity.

Instead, Casswell's main witness was Dr Hubert. Unfortunately, Casswell was unaware that the doctor was a drug addict. Hubert gave his evidence satisfactorily, but when it came to his cross-examination by the prosecution, Hawke managed to tie him up in knots to the point where, according to Hubert, it almost seemed that any criminal could claim to be insane and therefore free from responsibility for his crimes. To make matters worse, following Hubert's testimony, the prosecution immediately called two very believable medical witnesses who countered almost every point of his evidence.

In his summing up for the jury, Casswell tried valiantly to rescue his insanity defence, pointing out that, when viewed together, the two murders were evidence of insanity, as were Heath's lack of remorse, his inadequate steps to cover his tracks after the killings and his foolhardy voluntary contacts with the police after each murder. The jury retired on the third day of the trial, returning an hour later to pronounce Heath guilty.

When asked if he had anything to say as to why he should not receive sentence of death, Heath replied simply 'Nothing'. In the run-up to his execution, he decided not to allow his defence lawyers to appeal his sentence and refused all visitors, with the exception of his solicitor.

On 14 October 1946, the then Home Secretary, Mr Chuter Ede, declined to interfere with the death sentence imposed on Heath, in spite of a last-minute campaign by well-known death penalty abolitionist Mrs Violet Van der Elst, who claimed to have new evidence on the case. Mrs Van der Elst had spoken to Heath's mother and had learned that Heath had been brain damaged at birth – calling Heath a 'possessed madman'; Mrs Van der Elst insisted that he should have been sent to Broadmoor rather than the gallows. She was later arrested and charged with causing an obstruction, for distributing leaflets outside the prison at the time of Heath's execution, for which she was fined £2.

Her protests were in vain. On 16 October 1946, Heath kept his appointment with executioner Albert Pierrepoint at Pentonville Prison. While waiting to enter the execution chamber, an unconcerned Heath asked the prison governor for a whisky, immediately adding, 'You might as well make that a double.'

BIBLIOGRAPHY & REFERENCES

BOOKS

Browne, Douglas G. and Tullett, E.V., *Bernard Spilsbury: His Life and Cases*, George G. Harrap and Co. Ltd, 1951
Casswell QC, J.D., *A Lance for Liberty*, George G. Harrap and Co. Ltd, London, 1961
Eddleston, John J., *The Encyclopaedia of Executions*, John Blake, London, 2004
Guttridge, Roger, *Dorset Murders*, Roy Gasson Associates, 1986
Murphy, Theresa, *Murder in Dorset*, Robert Hale Ltd, 1988

NEWSPAPERS

Bournemouth Daily Echo
Dorset County Chronicle
Dorset County Chronicle & Somersetshire Gazette
Poole and East Dorset Herald
The Telegram
The Times

Certain websites have also been consulted in the compilation of this book, but since they have a habit of disappearing, to avoid frustration they have not been cited.

INDEX